www.EffortlessMath.com

... So Much More Online!

✓ FREE Math lessons

✓ More Math learning books!

✓ Mathematics Worksheets

✓ Online Math Tutors

Need a PDF version of this book?

Please visit www.EffortlessMath.com

PERT Math Full Study Guide

2023 - 2024

Comprehensive Review + Practice Tests + Online Resources

By

Reza Nazari

All inquiries should be addressed to:

info@effortlessMath.com

www.EffortlessMath.com

ISBN: 978-1-63719-114-9

Published by: Effortless Math Education Inc.

www.EffortlessMath.com

Visit www.EffortlessMath.com

for Online Math Practice

Welcome to

PERT Math Prep

2023

Thank you for choosing Effortless Math for your PERT Math test preparation and congratulations on making the decision to take the PERT test! It's a remarkable move you are taking, one that shouldn't be diminished in any capacity. That's why you need to use every tool possible to ensure you succeed on the test with the highest possible score, and this extensive study guide is one such tool.

If math has never been a strong subject for you, **don't worry**! This book will help you prepare for (and even ACE) the PERT test's math section. As test day draws nearer, effective preparation becomes increasingly more important. Thankfully, you have this comprehensive study guide to help you get ready for the test. With this guide, you can feel confident that you will be more than ready for the PERT Math test when the time comes.

First and foremost, it is important to note that this book is a study guide and not a textbook. It is best read from cover to cover. Every lesson of this "self-guided math book" was carefully developed to ensure that you are making the most effective use of your time while preparing for the test. This up-to-date guide reflects the 2023 test guidelines and will put you on the right track to hone your math skills, overcome exam anxiety, and boost your confidence, so that you can have your best to succeed on the PERT Math test.

This study guide will:

☑ Explain the format of the PERT Math test.

☑ Describe specific test-taking strategies that you can use on the test.

☑ Provide PERT Math test-taking tips.

☑ Review all PERT Math concepts and topics you will be tested on.

☑ Help you identify the areas in which you need to concentrate your study time.

☑ Offer exercises that help you develop the basic math skills you will learn in each section.

☑ Give **2 realistic and full-length practice tests** (featuring new question types) with detailed answers to help you measure your exam readiness and build confidence.

This resource contains everything you will ever need to succeed on the PERT Math test. You'll get in-depth instructions on every math topic as well as tips and techniques on how to answer each question type. You'll also get plenty of practice questions to boost your test-taking confidence.

In addition, in the following pages you'll find:

➢ **How to Use This Book Effectively** – This section provides you with step-by-step instructions on how to get the most out of this comprehensive study guide.

➢ **How to study for the PERT Math Test** – A six-step study program has been developed to help you make the best use of this book and prepare for your PERT Math test. Here you'll find tips and strategies to guide your study program and help you understand PERT Math and how to ace the test.

➢ **PERT Math Review** – Learn everything you need to know about the PERT Math test.

➢ **PERT Math Test-Taking Strategies** – Learn how to effectively put these recommended test-taking techniques into use for improving your PERT Math score.

➢ **Test Day Tips** – Review these tips to make sure you will do your best when the big day comes.

Effortless Math's PERT Online Center

Effortless Math Online PERT Center offers a complete study program, including the following:

✓ Step-by-step instructions on how to prepare for the PERT Math test

✓ Numerous PERT Math worksheets to help you measure your math skills

✓ Complete list of PERT Math formulas

✓ Video lessons for all PERT Math topics

✓ Full-length PERT Math practice tests

✓ And much more...

No Registration Required.

Visit **EffortlessMath.com/PERT** to find your online PERT Math resources.

How to Use This Book Effectively

Look no further when you need a study guide to improve your math skills to succeed on the math portion of the PERT test. Each chapter of this comprehensive guide to the PERT Math will provide you with the knowledge, tools, and understanding needed for every topic covered on the test.

It's imperative that you understand each topic before moving onto another one, as that's the way to guarantee your success. Each chapter provides you with examples and a step-by-step guide of every concept to better understand the content that will be on the test. To get the best possible results from this book:

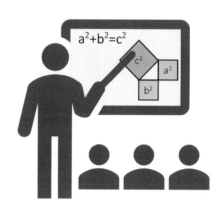

➤ **Begin studying long before your test date**. This provides you ample time to learn the different math concepts. The earlier you begin studying for the test, the sharper your skills will be. Do not procrastinate! Provide yourself with plenty of time to learn the concepts and feel comfortable that you understand them when your test date arrives.

➤ **Practice consistently**. Study PERT Math concepts at least 20 to 30 minutes a day. Remember, slow and steady wins the race, which can be applied to preparing for the PERT Math test. Instead of cramming to tackle everything at once, be patient and learn the math topics in short bursts.

➤ Whenever you get a math problem wrong, **mark it off, and review it later** to make sure you understand the concept.

➤ Start each session by **looking over the previous material.**

➤ Once you've reviewed the book's lessons, **take a practice test at the back of the book** to gauge your level of readiness. Then, review your results. Read detailed answers and solutions for each question you missed.

➤ **Take another practice test** to get an idea of how ready you are to take the actual exam. Taking the practice tests will give you the confidence you need on test day. Simulate the PERT testing environment by sitting in a quiet room free from distraction. Make sure to clock yourself with a timer.

How to Study for the PERT Math Test

Studying for the PERT Math test can be a really daunting and boring task. What's the best way to go about it? Is there a certain study method that works better than others? Well, studying for the PERT Math can be done effectively. The following six-step program has been designed to make preparing for the PERT Math test more efficient and less overwhelming.

Step 1 - Create a study plan
Step 2 - Choose your study resources
Step 3 - Review, Learn, Practice
Step 4 - Learn and practice test-taking strategies
Step 5 - Learn the PERT Test format and take practice tests
Step 6 - Analyze your performance

STEP 1: Create a Study Plan

It's always easier to get things done when you have a plan. Creating a study plan for the PERT Math test can help you to stay on track with your studies. It's important to sit down and prepare a study plan with what works with your life, work, and any other obligations you may have. Devote enough time each day to studying. It's also a great idea to break down each section of the exam into blocks and study one concept at a time.

It's important to understand that there is no "right" way to create a study plan. Your study plan will be personalized based on your specific needs and learning style.

Follow these guidelines to create an effective study plan for your PERT Math test:

★ **Analyze your learning style and study habits** – Everyone has a different learning style. It is essential to embrace your individuality and the unique way you learn. Think about what works and what doesn't work for you. Do you prefer PERT Math prep books or a combination of textbooks and video lessons? Does it work better for you if you study every night for thirty minutes or is it more effective to study in the morning before going to work?

★ **Evaluate your schedule** – Review your current schedule and find out how much time you can consistently devote to PERT Math study.

★ **Develop a schedule** – Now it's time to add your study schedule to your calendar like any other obligation. Schedule time for study, practice, and review. Plan out which topic you will study on which day to ensure that you're devoting enough time to each concept. Develop a study plan that is mindful, realistic, and flexible.

★ **Stick to your schedule** – A study plan is only effective when it is followed consistently. You should try to develop a study plan that you can follow for the length of your study program.

★ **Evaluate your study plan and adjust as needed** – Sometimes you need to adjust your plan when you have new commitments. Check in with yourself regularly to make sure that you're not falling behind in your study plan. Remember, the most important thing is sticking to your plan. Your study plan is all about helping you be more productive. If you find that your study plan is not as effective as you want, don't get discouraged. It's okay to make changes as you figure out what works best for you.

STEP 2: Choose Your Study Resources

There are numerous textbooks and online resources available for the PERT Math test, and it may not be clear where to begin. Don't worry! This study guide provides everything you need to fully prepare for your PERT Math test. In addition to the book content, you can also use Effortless Math's online resources. (video lessons, worksheets, formulas, etc.) On each

page, there is a link (and a QR code) to an online webpage which provides a comprehensive review of the topic, step-by-step instruction, video tutorial, and numerous examples and exercises to help you fully understand the concept.

You can also visit <u>EffortlessMath.com/PERT</u> to find your online PERT Math resources.

STEP 3: Review, Learn, Practice

This PERT Math study guide breaks down each subject into specific skills or content areas. For instance, the percent concept is separated into different topics–percent calculation, percent increase and decrease, percent problems, etc. Use this study guide and Effortless Math online PERT center to help you go over all key math concepts and topics on the PERT Math test.

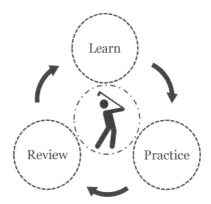

As you read each topic, take notes or highlight the concepts you would like to go over again in the future. If you're unfamiliar with a topic or something is difficult for you, use the link (or the QR code) at the bottom of the page to find the webpage that provides more instruction about that topic. For each math topic, plenty of instructions, step-by-step guides, and examples are provided to ensure you get a good grasp of the material.

Quickly review the topics you do understand to get a brush-up of the material. Be sure to do the practice questions provided at the end of every chapter to measure your understanding of the concepts.

STEP 4: Learn and Practice Test-taking Strategies

In the following sections, you will find important test-taking strategies and tips that can help you earn extra points. You'll learn how to think strategically and when to guess if you don't know the answer to a question. Using PERT Math test-taking strategies and tips can help you raise your score and do well on the test. Apply test taking strategies on the practice tests to help you boost your confidence.

STEP 5: Learn the PERT Test Format and Take Practice Tests

The PERT *Test Review* section provides information about the structure of the PERT test. Read this section to learn more about the PERT test structure, different test sections, the number of questions in each section, and the section time limits. When you have a prior understanding of the test format and different types of PERT Math questions, you'll feel more confident when you take the actual exam.

Once you have read through the instructions and lessons and feel like you are ready to go – take advantage of both of the full-length PERT Math practice tests available in this study guide. Use the practice tests to sharpen your skills and build confidence.

The PERT Math practice tests offered at the end of the book are formatted similarly to the actual PERT Math test. When you take each practice test, try to simulate actual testing conditions. To take the practice tests, sit in a quiet space, time yourself, and work through as many of the questions as time allows. The practice tests are followed by detailed answer explanations to help you find your weak areas, learn from your mistakes, and raise your PERT Math score.

STEP 6: Analyze Your Performance

After taking the practice tests, look over the answer keys and explanations to learn which questions you answered correctly and which you did not. Never be discouraged if you make a few mistakes. See them as a learning opportunity. This will highlight your strengths and weaknesses.

You can use the results to determine if you need additional practice or if you are ready to take the actual PERT Math test.

Looking for more?

Visit EffortlessMath.com/PERT to find hundreds of PERT Math worksheets, video tutorials, practice tests, PERT Math formulas, and much more.

Or scan this QR code.

No Registration Required.

PERT Test Review

The Postsecondary Education Readiness Test, is known as the PERT, is a test to determine the appropriate level of college course work for an incoming student. In essence, it is a broad and quick assessment of students' academic abilities.

The PERT test consists of three multiple-choice separate exams:

- Mathematics
- Reading
- Writing

The PERT test is a Computer Adaptive Test (CAT). It means that if the correct answer is chosen, the next question will be harder. If the answer given is incorrect, the next question will be easier. This also means that once an answer is selected on the CAT it cannot be changed.

The mathematics portion of the PERT test contains 30 multiple-choice questions. The test covers data analysis, geometry, and algebra on both intermediate and basic levels. The topics on the math test includes:

- linear equations, linear inequalities, literal equation, and quadratic formulas
- simultaneous linear equations with two variables
- evaluating algebraic expressions
- translating between lines and inspecting equations on coordinate planes
- dividing by binomials and monomials
- adding, subtracting, multiplying, dividing, simplifying and factoring polynomial

Students are not allowed to use calculator when taking a PERT assessment. A pop-up calculator is embedded in the test for some questions. Scores on the PERT test range from 50 to 150. On the PERT mathematics exam, you will be placed in lower-level developmental education if you score between 50-95. If your score is between 96 and 113, then you will be placed in higher level developmental education. A score of 114 to 122 will enable you to be place in Intermediate Algebra (MAT 1033). Score of 123 or higher will allow you to take College Algebra or higher (MAC 1105).

PERT Math Test-Taking Strategies

Here are some test-taking strategies that you can use to maximize your performance and results on the PERT Math test.

#1 : USE THIS APPROACH TO ANSWER EVERY PERT MATH QUESTION

- Review the question to identify keywords and important information.
- Translate the keywords into math operations so you can solve the problem.
- Review the answer choices. What are the differences between answer choices?
- Draw or label a diagram if needed.
- Try to find patterns.
- Find the right method to answer the question. Use straightforward math, plug in numbers, or test the answer choices (backsolving).
- Double-check your work.

#2 : USE EDUCATED GUESSING

This approach is applicable to the problems you understand to some degree but cannot solve using straightforward math. In such cases, try to filter out as many answer choices as possible before picking an answer. In cases where you don't have a clue about what a certain problem entails, don't waste any time trying to eliminate answer choices. Just choose one randomly before moving onto the next question.

As you can ascertain, direct solutions are the most optimal approach. Carefully read through the question, determine what the solution is using the math you have learned before, then coordinate the answer with one of the choices available to you. Are you stumped? Make your best guess, then move on.

Don't leave any fields empty! Even if you're unable to work out a problem, strive to answer it. Take a guess if you have to. You will not lose points by getting an answer wrong, though you may gain a point by getting it correct!

#3 : Ballpark

A ballpark answer is a rough approximation. When we become overwhelmed by calculations and figures, we end up making silly mistakes. A decimal that is moved by one unit can change an answer from right to wrong, regardless of the number of steps that you went through to get it. That's where ballparking can play a big part.

If you think you know what the correct answer may be (even if it's just a ballpark answer), you'll usually have the ability to eliminate a couple of choices. While answer choices are usually based on the average student error and/or values that are closely tied, you will still be able to weed out choices that are way far afield. Try to find answers that aren't in the proverbial ballpark when you're looking for a wrong answer on a multiple-choice question. This is an optimal approach to eliminating answers to a problem.

#4 : Backsolving

All questions on the PERT Math test will be in multiple-choice format. Many test-takers prefer multiple-choice questions, as at least the answer is right there. You'll typically have four answers to pick from. You simply need to figure out which one is correct. Usually, the best way to go about doing so is "backsolving."

As mentioned earlier, direct solutions are the most optimal approach to answering a question. Carefully read through a problem, calculate a solution, then correspond the answer with one of the choices displayed in front of you. If you can't calculate a solution, your next best approach involves "backsolving."

When backsolving a problem, contrast one of your answer options against the problem you are asked, then see which of them is most relevant. More often than not, answer choices are listed in ascending or descending order. In such cases, try out the choices B or C. If it's not correct, you can go either down or up from there.

#5 : PLUGGING IN NUMBERS

"Plugging in numbers" is a strategy that can be applied to a wide range of different math problems on the PERT Math test. This approach is typically used to simplify a challenging question so that it is more understandable. By using the strategy carefully, you can find the answer without too much trouble.

The concept is fairly straightforward–replace unknown variables in a problem with certain values. When selecting a number, consider the following:

- Choose a number that's basic (just not too basic). Generally, you should avoid choosing 1 (or even 0). A decent choice is 2.

- Try not to choose a number that is displayed in the problem.

- Make sure you keep your numbers different if you need to choose at least two of them.

- More often than not, choosing numbers merely lets you filter out some of your answer choices. As such, don't just go with the first choice that gives you the right answer.

- If several answers seem correct, then you'll need to choose another value and try again. This time, though, you'll just need to check choices that haven't been eliminated yet.

- If your question contains fractions, then a potential right answer may involve either an LCD (least common denominator) or an LCD multiple.

- 100 is the number you should choose when you are dealing with problems involving percentages.

PERT Mathematics Test – Daytime Tips

After practicing and reviewing all the math concepts you've been taught, and taking some PERT mathematics practice tests, you'll be prepared for test day. Consider the following tips to be extra-ready come test time.

Before Your Test

What to do the night before:

- **Relax!** One day before your test, study lightly or skip studying altogether. You shouldn't attempt to learn something new, either. There are plenty of reasons why studying the evening before a big test can work against you. Put it this way–a marathoner wouldn't go out for a sprint before the day of a big race. Mental marathoners–such as yourself–should not study for any more than one hour 24 hours before a PERT test. That's because your brain requires some rest to be at its best. The night before your exam, spend some time with family or friends, or read a book.

- **Avoid bright screens** - You'll have to get some good shuteye the night before your test. Bright screens (such as the ones coming from your laptop, TV, or mobile device) should be avoided altogether. Staring at such a screen will keep your brain up, making it hard to drift asleep at a reasonable hour.

- **Make sure your dinner is healthy** - The meal that you have for dinner should be nutritious. Be sure to drink plenty of water as well. Load up on your complex carbohydrates, much like a marathon runner would do. Pasta, rice, and potatoes are ideal options here, as are vegetables and protein sources.

- **Get your bag ready for test day** - The night prior to your test, pack your bag with your stationery, admissions pass, ID, and any other gear that you need. Keep the bag right by your front door.

- **Make plans to reach the testing site** - Before going to sleep, ensure that you understand precisely how you will arrive at the site of the test. If parking is something you'll have to find first, plan for it. If you're dependent on public transit, then review the schedule. You should also make sure that the train/bus/subway/streetcar you use will be running. Find out about road closures

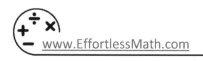

as well. If a parent or friend is accompanying you, ensure that they understand what steps they have to take as well.

The Day of the Test

■ **Get up reasonably early, but not too early.**

■ **Have breakfast** - Breakfast improves your concentration, memory, and mood. As such, make sure the breakfast that you eat in the morning is healthy. The last thing you want to be is distracted by a grumbling tummy. If it's not your own stomach making those noises, another test taker close to you might be instead. Prevent discomfort or embarrassment by consuming a healthy breakfast. Bring a snack with you if you think you'll need it.

■ **Follow your daily routine** - Do you watch Good Morning America each morning while getting ready for the day? Don't break your usual habits on the day of the test. Likewise, if coffee isn't something you drink in the morning, then don't take up the habit hours before your test. Routine consistency lets you concentrate on the main objective–doing the best you can on your test.

■ **Wear layers** - Dress yourself up in comfortable layers. You should be ready for any kind of internal temperature. If it gets too warm during the test, take a layer off.

■ **Get there on time** - The last thing you want to do is get to the test site late. Rather, you should be there 45 minutes prior to the start of the test. Upon your arrival, try not to hang out with anybody who is nervous. Any anxious energy they exhibit shouldn't influence you.

■ **Leave the books at home** - No books should be brought to the test site. If you start developing anxiety before the test, books could encourage you to do some last-minute studying, which will only hinder you. Keep the books far away–better yet, leave them at home.

■ **Make your voice heard** - If something is off, speak to a proctor. If medical attention is needed or if you'll require anything, consult the proctor prior to the start of the test. Any doubts you have should be clarified. You should be entering the test site with a state of mind that is completely clear.

- **Have faith in yourself** - When you feel confident, you will be able to perform at your best. When you are waiting for the test to begin, envision yourself receiving an outstanding result. Try to see yourself as someone who knows all the answers, no matter what the questions are. A lot of athletes tend to use this technique–particularly before a big competition. Your expectations will be reflected by your performance.

During your test

- **Be calm and breathe deeply** - You need to relax before the test, and some deep breathing will go a long way to help you do that. Be confident and calm. You got this. Everybody feels a little stressed out just before an evaluation of any kind is set to begin. Learn some effective breathing exercises. Spend a minute meditating before the test starts. Filter out any negative thoughts you have. Exhibit confidence when having such thoughts.

- **Concentrate on the test** - Refrain from comparing yourself to anyone else. You shouldn't be distracted by the people near you or random noise. Concentrate exclusively on the test. If you find yourself irritated by surrounding noises, earplugs can be used to block sounds off close to you. Don't forget–the test is going to last several hours if you're taking more than one subject of the test. Some of that time will be dedicated to brief sections. Concentrate on the specific section you are working on during a particular moment. Do not let your mind wander off to upcoming or previous sections.

- **Try to answer each question individually** - Focus only on the question you are working on. Use one of the test-taking strategies to solve the problem. If you aren't able to come up with an answer, don't get frustrated. Simply skip that question, then move onto the next one.

- **Don't forget to breathe!** Whenever you notice your mind wandering, your stress levels boosting, or frustration brewing, take a thirty-second break. Shut your eyes, drop your pencil, breathe deeply, and let your shoulders relax. You will end up being more productive when you allow yourself to relax for a moment.

- **Optimize your breaks** - When break time comes, use the restroom, have a snack, and reactivate your energy for the subsequent section. Doing some stretches can help stimulate your blood flow.

After your test

- **Take it easy** - You will need to set some time aside to relax and decompress once the test has concluded. There is no need to stress yourself out about what you could've said, or what you may have done wrong. At this point, there's nothing you can do about it. Your energy and time would be better spent on something that will bring you happiness for the remainder of your day.

- **Redoing the test** - Did you pass the test? Congratulations! Your hard work paid off!

  If you have failed your test, though, don't worry! The test can be retaken. In such cases, you will need to follow the retake policy. You also need to re-register to take the exam again.

Contents

CHAPTER

1

Fractions and Mixed Numbers

Math topics that you'll learn in this chapter:

- ✓ Simplifying Fractions
- ✓ Adding and Subtracting Fractions
- ✓ Multiplying and Dividing Fractions
- ✓ Adding Mixed Numbers
- ✓ Subtracting Mixed Numbers
- ✓ Multiplying Mixed Numbers
- ✓ Dividing Mixed Numbers

1

Topic	Simplifying Fractions
Notes	✓ Evenly divide both the top and bottom of the fraction by $2, 3, 5, 7, \ldots$ etc. ✓ Continue until you can't go any further.
Example	**Simplify** $\dfrac{72}{96}$ To simplify $\dfrac{72}{96}$, find a number that both 72 and 96 are divisible by. Both are divisible by 24. Then: $\dfrac{72}{96} = \dfrac{72 \div 24}{96 \div 24} = \dfrac{3}{4}$

Your Turn!	1) $\dfrac{4}{12} =$	2) $\dfrac{11}{44} =$
	3) $\dfrac{13}{39} =$	4) $\dfrac{12}{48} =$
	5) $\dfrac{14}{63} =$	6) $\dfrac{20}{120} =$
	7) $\dfrac{27}{72} =$	8) $\dfrac{36}{96} =$
	9) $\dfrac{35}{65} =$	10) $\dfrac{36}{88} =$

Find more at

bit.ly/3nOGNko

Topic	**Adding and Subtracting Fractions**
Notes	✓ For "like" fractions (fractions with the same denominator), add or subtract the numerators and write the answer over the common denominator. ✓ Find equivalent fractions with the same denominator before you can add or subtract fractions with different denominators. ✓ Adding and Subtracting with the same denominator: $$\frac{a}{b} + \frac{c}{b} = \frac{a+c}{b}, \frac{a}{b} - \frac{c}{b} = \frac{a-c}{b}$$ ✓ Adding and Subtracting fractions with different denominators: $$\frac{a}{b} + \frac{c}{d} = \frac{ad+bc}{bd}, \frac{a}{b} - \frac{c}{d} = \frac{ad-bc}{bd}$$
Example	***Find the sum.*** $\frac{1}{3} + \frac{2}{5} =$ For "unlike" fractions, find equivalent fractions with the same denominator before you can add fractions with different denominators. Use this formula: $\frac{a}{b} + \frac{c}{b} =$ $$\frac{a+c}{b} \rightarrow \frac{(5)(1)+(3)(2)}{3 \times 5} = \frac{11}{15}$$ ***Subtract.*** $\frac{6}{5} - \frac{3}{5}$ For like fractions, subtract and write the answer over the common denominator: $$\frac{6-3}{5} = \frac{3}{5}$$
Your Turn! **Find more at** bit.ly/3nKet2X	1) $\frac{2}{7} + \frac{3}{7} =$ 　　　　　 2) $\frac{7}{8} - \frac{1}{4} =$ 3) $\frac{4}{5} + \frac{1}{9} =$ 　　　　　 4) $\frac{3}{7} - \frac{1}{4} =$ 5) $\frac{2}{9} + \frac{3}{4} =$ 　　　　　 6) $\frac{5}{6} - \frac{2}{5} =$ 7) $\frac{1}{3} + \frac{3}{8} =$ 　　　　　 8) $\frac{9}{11} - \frac{2}{3} =$

Topic	**Multiplying and Dividing Fractions**
Notes	✓ Multiplying fractions: multiply the top numbers and multiply the bottom numbers. ✓ Dividing fractions: Keep, Change, Flip Keep first fraction, change division sign to multiplication, and flip the numerator and denominator of the second fraction. Then, solve!
Examples	***Multiply.*** $\frac{2}{7} \times \frac{1}{6} =$ Multiply the top numbers and multiply the bottom numbers. $\frac{2}{7} \times \frac{1}{6} = \frac{2 \times 1}{7 \times 6} = \frac{2}{42}$, simplify: $\frac{2}{42} = \frac{2 \div 2}{42 \div 2} = \frac{1}{21}$ ***Divide.*** $\frac{2}{6} \div \frac{2}{3} =$ Keep first fraction, change division sign to multiplication, and flip the numerator and denominator of the second fraction. Then: $\frac{2}{6} \div \frac{2}{3} = \frac{2}{6} \times \frac{3}{2} = \frac{2 \times 3}{6 \times 2} = \frac{6 \div 6}{12 \div 6} = \frac{1}{2}$
Your Turn!	1) $\frac{3}{4} \times \frac{2}{3} =$ 2) $\frac{3}{8} \div \frac{2}{3} =$
	3) $\frac{3}{8} \times \frac{4}{5} =$ 4) $\frac{4}{5} \div \frac{4}{15} =$
	5) $\frac{1}{8} \times \frac{3}{7} =$ 6) $\frac{5}{9} \div \frac{4}{7} =$
Find more at bit.ly/3haSiQW	7) $\frac{2}{15} \times \frac{3}{8} =$ 8) $\frac{1}{9} \div \frac{5}{6} =$

Topic	Adding Mixed Numbers
Notes	Use the following steps for adding mixed numbers. ✓ Add whole numbers of the mixed numbers. ✓ Add the fractions of each mixed number. ✓ Find the Least Common Denominator (LCD) if necessary. ✓ Add whole numbers and fractions. ✓ Write your answer in lowest terms.
Example	***Add mixed numbers.*** $1\frac{1}{2} + 2\frac{2}{3} =$ Rewriting our equation with parts separated, $1 + \frac{1}{2} + 2 + \frac{2}{3}$ Add whole numbers: $1 + 2 = 3$ Add fractions: $\frac{1}{2} + \frac{2}{3} = \frac{3}{6} + \frac{4}{6} = \frac{7}{6} = 1\frac{1}{6}$, Now, combine the whole and fraction parts: $3 + 1 + \frac{1}{6} = 4\frac{1}{6}$
Your Turn!	1) $9\frac{1}{2} + 5\frac{3}{4} =$ 2) $4\frac{3}{2} + 2\frac{1}{6} =$
	3) $6\frac{3}{4} + 3\frac{5}{28} =$ 4) $4\frac{2}{5} + 6\frac{2}{4} =$
	5) $4\frac{6}{7} + 5\frac{3}{5} =$ 6) $3\frac{1}{6} + 1\frac{2}{7} =$
Find more at bit.ly/2M4oABB	7) $4\frac{5}{9} + 2\frac{2}{7} =$ 8) $7\frac{1}{9} + 5\frac{2}{6} =$

Topic	**Subtracting Mixed Numbers**
Notes	Use the following steps for subtracting mixed numbers. ✓ Convert mixed numbers into improper fractions. $a\frac{c}{b} = \frac{ab+c}{b}$ ✓ Find equivalent fractions with the same denominator for unlike fractions (fractions with different denominators) ✓ Subtract the second fraction from the first one. ✓ Write your answer in lowest terms and convert it into a mixed number if the answer is an improper fraction.
Example	**Subtract.** $9\frac{1}{2} - 5\frac{1}{4} =$ Convert mixed numbers into fractions: $9\frac{1}{2} = \frac{9\times2+1}{2} = \frac{19}{2}$ and $5\frac{1}{4} = \frac{5\times4+1}{4} = \frac{21}{4}$, these two fractions are "unlike" fractions. (they have different denominators). Find equivalent fractions with the same denominator. Use this formula: $\frac{a}{b} - \frac{c}{d} = \frac{ad-bc}{bd}$ $\frac{19}{2} - \frac{21}{4} = \frac{(19)(4)-(21)(2)}{2\times4} = \frac{76-42}{8} = \frac{34}{8}$, the answer is an improper fraction, convert it into a mixed number. $\frac{34}{8} = 4\frac{2}{8} = 4\frac{1}{4}$
Your Turn! **Find more at** bit.ly/3aD3KDG	1) $3\frac{3}{4} - 1\frac{1}{2} =$

1) $3\frac{3}{4} - 1\frac{1}{2} =$	2) $2\frac{4}{9} - 1\frac{2}{3} =$
3) $5\frac{1}{6} - 2\frac{5}{12} =$	4) $5\frac{1}{3} - 1\frac{3}{4} =$
5) $4\frac{5}{6} - 1\frac{1}{8} =$	6) $7\frac{3}{4} - 1\frac{2}{3} =$
7) $9\frac{5}{6} - 5\frac{1}{5} =$	8) $4\frac{1}{4} - 3\frac{7}{9} =$

Topic	Multiplying Mixed Numbers
Notes	✓ Convert the mixed numbers into fractions. $a\frac{c}{b} = a + \frac{c}{b} = \frac{ab+c}{b}$ ✓ Multiply fractions and simplify if necessary. $\frac{a}{b} \times \frac{c}{d} = \frac{a \times c}{b \times d}$ ✓ If the answer is an improper fraction (numerator is bigger than denominator), convert it into a mixed number.
Example	**Multiply** $2\frac{1}{2} \times 4\frac{1}{3}$ Convert mixed numbers into fractions: $2\frac{1}{2} = \frac{2 \times 2 + 1}{2} = \frac{5}{2}$ and $4\frac{1}{3} = \frac{4 \times 3 + 1}{3} = \frac{13}{3}$ Multiply two fractions: $\frac{5}{2} \times \frac{13}{3} = \frac{5 \times 13}{2 \times 3} = \frac{65}{6}$ The answer is an improper fraction. Convert it into a mixed number: $$\frac{65}{6} = 10\frac{5}{6}$$
Your Turn!	1) $2\frac{2}{3} \times 1\frac{2}{3} =$ 2) $4\frac{1}{5} \times 2\frac{2}{3} =$ 3) $3\frac{3}{5} \times 3\frac{2}{3} =$ 4) $3\frac{1}{2} \times 4\frac{1}{3} =$ 5) $5\frac{3}{4} \times 2\frac{1}{5} =$ 6) $6\frac{3}{7} \times 9\frac{1}{4} =$ 7) $4\frac{4}{5} \times 3\frac{2}{3} =$ 8) $5\frac{1}{6} \times 3\frac{1}{4} =$

Find more at

bit.ly/3aPy7XJ

Topic	Dividing Mixed Numbers
Notes	✓ Convert the mixed numbers into improper fractions. $$a\frac{c}{b} = a + \frac{c}{b} = \frac{ab+c}{b}$$ ✓ Divide fractions and simplify if necessary.
Example	**Solve.** $1\frac{1}{2} \div 3\frac{1}{8} =$ Converting mixed numbers to fractions: $1\frac{1}{2} \div 3\frac{1}{8} = \frac{3}{2} \div \frac{25}{8}$ Keep, Change, Flip: $\frac{3}{2} \div \frac{25}{8} = \frac{3}{2} \times \frac{8}{25} = \frac{3\times 8}{2\times 25} = \frac{24}{50} = \frac{12}{25}$

Your Turn!	1) $6\frac{1}{2} \div 2\frac{1}{4} =$	2) $3\frac{1}{3} \div 2\frac{3}{5} =$
	3) $2\frac{3}{4} \div 1\frac{1}{2} =$	4) $6\frac{2}{3} \div 4\frac{3}{4} =$
	5) $1\frac{1}{3} \div 8\frac{2}{3} =$	6) $8\frac{1}{4} \div 4\frac{1}{2} =$
	7) $2\frac{4}{5} \div 3\frac{2}{9} =$	8) $8\frac{3}{4} \div 2\frac{5}{8} =$
Find more at bit.ly/2KLPk9k	9) $4\frac{1}{6} \div 2\frac{5}{3} =$	10) $4\frac{3}{8} \div 4\frac{1}{4} =$

Chapter 1: Answers

Simplifying Fractions

1) $\frac{1}{3}$

2) $\frac{1}{4}$

3) $\frac{1}{3}$

4) $\frac{1}{4}$

5) $\frac{2}{9}$

6) $\frac{1}{6}$

7) $\frac{3}{8}$

8) $\frac{3}{8}$

9) $\frac{7}{13}$

10) $\frac{9}{22}$

Adding and Subtracting Fractions

1) $\frac{5}{7}$

2) $\frac{5}{8}$

3) $\frac{41}{45}$

4) $\frac{5}{28}$

5) $\frac{35}{36}$

6) $\frac{13}{30}$

7) $\frac{17}{24}$

8) $\frac{5}{33}$

Multiplying and Dividing Fractions

1) $\frac{1}{2}$

2) $\frac{9}{16}$

3) $\frac{3}{10}$

4) 3

5) $\frac{3}{56}$

6) $\frac{35}{36}$

7) $\frac{1}{20}$

8) $\frac{2}{15}$

Adding Mixed Numbers

1) $15\frac{1}{4}$

2) $7\frac{2}{3}$

3) $9\frac{13}{14}$

4) $10\frac{9}{10}$

5) $10\frac{16}{35}$

6) $4\frac{19}{42}$

7) $6\frac{53}{63}$

8) $12\frac{4}{9}$

Subtracting Mixed Numbers

1) $2\frac{1}{4}$

2) $\frac{7}{9}$

3) $2\frac{3}{4}$

4) $3\frac{7}{12}$

5) $3\frac{17}{24}$

6) $6\frac{1}{12}$

7) $4\frac{19}{30}$

8) $\frac{17}{36}$

Multiplying Mixed Numbers

1) $4\frac{4}{9}$

2) $11\frac{1}{5}$

3) $13\frac{1}{5}$

4) $15\frac{1}{16}$

5) $12\frac{13}{20}$

6) $59\frac{13}{28}$

7) $17\frac{3}{5}$

8) $16\frac{19}{24}$

Dividing Mixed Numbers

1) $2\frac{8}{9}$

2) $1\frac{11}{39}$

3) $1\frac{5}{6}$

4) $1\frac{23}{57}$

5) $\frac{2}{13}$

6) $1\frac{5}{6}$

7) $\frac{126}{145}$

8) $3\frac{1}{3}$

9) $1\frac{3}{22}$

10) $1\frac{1}{34}$

CHAPTER

2 Decimals

Math topics that you'll learn in this chapter:

- ✓ Comparing Decimals
- ✓ Rounding Decimals
- ✓ Adding and Subtracting Decimals
- ✓ Multiplying and Dividing Decimals

11

Topic	**Comparing Decimals**
Notes	Decimals: is a fraction written in a special form. For example, instead of writing $\frac{1}{2}$ you can write **0.5**. For comparing decimals: ✓ Compare each digit of two decimals in the same place value. ✓ Start from left. Compare hundreds, tens, ones, tenth, hundredth, etc. ✓ To compare numbers, use these symbols: - Equal to =, Less than <, Greater than > Greater than or equal ≥, Less than or equal ≤
Examples	*Compare **0.60 and 0.06**.* 0.60 is greater than 0.06, because the tenth place of 0.60 is 6, but the tenth place of 0.06 is zero. Then: 0.60 > 0.06 *Compare **0.0751 and 0.751**.* 0.751 is greater than 0.0751, because the tenth place of 0.751 is 7, but the tenth place of 0.0751 is zero. Then: 0.0751 < 0.751
Your Turn!	1) 0.44 ☐ 0.48 2) 1.23 ☐ 1.30
	3) 15.55 ☐ 18.08 4) 2.57 ☐ 2.058
	5) 1.356 ☐ 13.56 6) 0.73 ☐ 0.730
Find more at bit.ly/2WHt2Za	7) 3.689 ☐ 3.698 8) 0.652 ☐ 0.625

Topic	**Rounding Decimals**
Notes	✓ We can round decimals to a certain accuracy or number of decimal places. ✓ Let's review place values: For example: 35.4817 3: tens 5: ones 4: tenths 8: hundredths 1: thousandths 7: tens thousandths ✓ To round a decimal, find the place value you'll round to. ✓ Find the digit to the right of the place value you're rounding to. If it is 5 or bigger, add 1 to the place value you're rounding to and remove all digits on its right side. If the digit to the right of the place value is less than 5, keep the place value and remove all digits on the right.
Example	***Round 11.7268 to the hundredth-place value.*** First look at the next place value to the right, (thousandths). It's 6 and it is greater than 5. Thus add 1 to the digit in the hundredth place. It is 2. → $2 + 1 = 3$, then, the answer is 11.73

Your Turn!	*Round each number to the underlined place value.*

1) $22.5\underline{66} =$	2) $1.3\underline{2}5 =$
3) $52.\underline{4}26 =$	4) $3\underline{5}.72 =$
5) $10.\underline{2}59 =$	6) $32.5\underline{06} =$
7) $6.4\underline{81} =$	8) $8.0\underline{1}9 =$

Find more at

bit.ly/3mKEluf

Topic	**Adding and Subtracting Decimals**
Notes	✓ Line up the numbers. ✓ Add zeros to have same number of digits for both numbers if necessary. ✓ Add or subtract using column addition or subtraction.
Examples	**Add**. $3.8 + 5.14 =$ First line up the numbers: $\begin{array}{r} 3.8 \\ +5.14 \\ \hline \end{array}$ →Add zeros to have same number of digits for both numbers. $\begin{array}{r} 3.80 \\ +5.14 \\ \hline \end{array}$ → Start with the hundredths place. $0 + 4 = 4$, $\begin{array}{r} 3.80 \\ +5.14 \\ \hline 4 \end{array}$ → Continue with tenths place. $8 + 1 = 9$, $\begin{array}{r} 3.80 \\ +5.14 \\ \hline .94 \end{array}$ → Add the ones place. $3 + 5 = 8$, $\begin{array}{r} 3.80 \\ +5.14 \\ \hline 8.94 \end{array}$ **Subtract**. $6.56 - 4.13 =$ $\begin{array}{r} 6.56 \\ -4.13 \\ \hline \end{array}$ Start with the hundredths place. $6 - 3 = 3$, $\begin{array}{r} 6.56 \\ -4.13 \\ \hline 3 \end{array}$, continue with tenths place. $5 - 1 = 4$, $\begin{array}{r} 6.56 \\ -4.13 \\ \hline .43 \end{array}$, subtract the ones place. $6 - 4 = 2$, $\begin{array}{r} 6.56 \\ -4.13 \\ \hline 2.43 \end{array}$
Your Turn!	1) $26.20 + 11.55 =$ 2) $62.25 - 26.10 =$
	3) $39.61 + 26.12 =$ 4) $55.58 - 42.26 =$
Find more at bit.ly/38uyUdx	5) $29.23 + 33.58 =$ 6) $33.48 - 24.40 =$

Topic	**Multiplying and Dividing Decimals**
Notes	For Multiplication: ✓ Ignore the decimal point and set up and multiply the numbers as you do with whole numbers. ✓ Count the total number of decimal places in both factors. ✓ Place the decimal point in the product. For Division: ✓ If the divisor is not a whole number, move decimal point to right to make it a whole number. Do the same for dividend. ✓ Divide similar to whole numbers.
Examples	***Find the product.*** $1.4 \times 2.6 =$ Set up and multiply the numbers as you do with whole numbers. Line up the numbers: $\begin{matrix}14\\ \times 26\end{matrix}$ → Multiply: $\begin{matrix}14\\ \times 26\\ \hline 364\end{matrix}$ → Count the total number of decimal places in both of the factors. There are two decimal digits. Then: $1.4 \times 2.6 = 3.64$ ***Find the quotient.*** $4.8 \div 0.6 =$ The divisor is not a whole number. Multiply it by 10 to get 6. → $0.6 \times 10 = 6$ Do the same for the dividend to get 48 → $4.8 \times 10 = 48$ Now, divide: $48 \div 6 = 8$. The answer is 8.

Your Turn! **Find more at** bit.ly/34DZ0cS	1) $1.24 \times 0.2 =$	2) $56.8 \div 0.2 =$
	3) $0.8 \times 0.42 =$	4) $36.6 \div 0.6 =$
	5) $0.25 \times 0.5 =$	6) $26.8 \div 100 =$

Chapter 2: Answers

Comparing Decimals

1) $<$
2) $<$
3) $<$

4) $>$
5) $<$
6) $=$

7) $<$
8) $>$

Rounding Decimals

1) 22.57
2) 1.33
3) 52.4

4) 40
5) 10.3
6) 32.51

7) 6.48
8) 8.02

Adding and Subtracting Decimals

1) 37.75
2) 36.15

3) 65.73
4) 13.32

5) 62.81
6) 9.08

Multiplying and Dividing Decimals

1) 0.248
2) 284

3) 0.336
4) 61

5) 0.125
6) 0.268

CHAPTER

3

Integers and Order of Operations

Math topics that you'll learn in this chapter:

- ✓ Adding and Subtracting Integers
- ✓ Multiplying and Dividing Integers
- ✓ Order of Operations
- ✓ Integers and Absolute Value

17

Topic	**Adding and Subtracting Integers**
Notes	✓ Integers include: zero, counting numbers, and the negative of the counting numbers. $\{..., -3, -2, -1, 0, 1, 2, 3, ...\}$ ✓ Add a positive integer by moving to the right on the number line. ✓ Add a negative integer by moving to the left on the number line. Subtract an integer by adding its opposite.
Examples	**Solve.** $(5) - (-3) =$ Keep the first number and convert the sign of the second number to its opposite. (change subtraction into addition. Then: $(5) + 3 = 8$ **Solve.** $48 + (20 - 34) =$ First subtract the numbers in brackets, $20 - 34 = -14$ Then: $48 + (-14) = \rightarrow$ change addition into subtraction: $48 - 14 = 34$

Your Turn!

1) $-(15) + 10 =$	2) $(-9) + (-12) =$
3) $-(-16) + 3 =$	4) $5 - (-2) + 11 =$
5) $(-4) + (-6) + 2 =$	6) $19 - (-2 + 6) =$
7) $-7 + (-14) + 9 =$	8) $-(20) - (-3) + 8 =$

Find more at

bit.ly/3aKx5vl

Topic	**Multiplying and Dividing Integers**
Notes	Use following rules for multiplying and dividing integers: ✓ (negative) × (negative) = positive ✓ (negative) ÷ (negative) = positive ✓ (negative) × (positive) = negative ✓ (negative) ÷ (positive) = negative ✓ (positive) × (positive) = positive ✓ (positive) ÷ (negative) = negative
Examples	**Solve.** $6 \times (11 - 5) =$ First subtract the numbers in brackets, $11 - 5 = 6 \rightarrow (6) \times (6) =$ Now use this rule: (positive) × (positive) = positive $(6) \times (6) = 36$ **Solve.** $(-36) + (-25 \div 5) =$ First divide -25 by 5 , the numbers in brackets, using this rule: (negative) ÷ (positive) = negative Then: $-25 \div 5 = -5$. Now, add -36 and -5: $$(-36) + (-5) = -36 - 5 = -41$$

Your Turn!	1) $(-7) \times 3 =$	2) $(-56) \div (8) =$
	3) $(-14) \times (-4) =$	4) $-63 \div (-9) =$
	5) $(18 - 11) \times (-6) =$	6) $(-15) \div (3 - 6) =$
Find more at bit.ly/3pjQW98	7) $8 \times (-7 + 6) =$	8) $(24) \div (-3 - 5) =$

Topic	Order of Operation
Notes	When there is more than one math operation, use PEMDAS: (to memorize this rule, remember the phrase "Please Excuse My Dear Aunt Sally") ✓ Parentheses ✓ Exponents ✓ Multiplication and Division (from left to right) ✓ Addition and Subtraction (from left to right)
Examples	***Calculate.*** $(18 - 26) \div (2^3 \div 4) =$ First simplify inside parentheses: $(-8) \div (8 \div 4) = (-8) \div (2)$ Then: $(-8) \div (2) = -4$ ***Solve.*** $(-6 \times 7) - (14 - 3^2) =$ First calculate within parentheses: $(-6 \times 7) - (14 - 3^2) = (-42) - (14 - 9)$ Then: $(-42) - (14 - 9) = -42 - 5 = -47$

Your Turn!	1) $(11 \times 3) \div (6 + 5) =$	2) $(32 \div 4) + (12 - 5) =$
	3) $(-23) + (5 \times 3) + 10 =$	4) $(-10 \times 9) \div (2^3 + 1) =$
Find more at	5) $[-14(48 \div 2^4)] \div 7 =$	6) $(-5) + (63 \div 3^2) + 11 =$
bit.ly/37LBw7X	7) $[15(72 \div 6^2)] - 4^2 =$	8) $4^3 + (-5 \times 2^4) + 18 =$

Topic	Integers and Absolute Value
Notes	✓ The absolute value of a number is its distance from zero, in either direction, on the number line. For example, the distance of 9 and -9 from zero on number line is 9. ✓ Absolute value is symbolized by vertical bars, as in $|x|$.
Example	**Calculate.** $\|8 - 3\| \times \|11 - 15\| =$ First calculate $\|8 - 3\|$, $\rightarrow \|8 - 3\| = \|5\|$, the absolute value of 5 is 5, $\|5\| = 5$ $5 \times \|11 - 15\| =$ Now calculate $\|11 - 15\|$, $\rightarrow \|11 - 15\| = \|-4\|$, the absolute value of -4 is 4, $\|-4\| = 4$. Then: $5 \times 4 = 20$

Your Turn!		
	1) $11 - \|7 - 12\| =$	2) $14 - \|10 - 15\| - \|9\| =$
	3) $\|28\| - \dfrac{\|-35\|}{7} =$	4) $\|-19\| + \dfrac{\|-48\|}{6} =$
	5) $\dfrac{\|4 \times -7\|}{4} \times \dfrac{\|-22\|}{2} =$	6) $\dfrac{\|10 \times -4\|}{5} \times \|-20\| =$
Find more at bit.ly/3aD521u	7) $\dfrac{\|-54\|}{9} \times \dfrac{\|-49\|}{7} =$	8) $\|-38 + 9\| \times \dfrac{\|-9 \times 4\|}{6} =$

Chapter 3: Answers

Adding and Subtracting Integers

1) −5   4) 18   7) −12
2) −21   5) −8   8) −9
3) 19   6) 15

Multiplying and Dividing Integers

1) −21   4) 7   7) −8
2) −7   5) −42   8) −3
3) 56   6) 5

Order of Operations

1) 3   4) −10   7) 14
2) 15   5) −6   8) 2
3) 2   6) 13

Integers and Absolute Values

1) 6   4) 27   7) 42
2) 0   5) 77   8) 174
3) 23   6) 160

4 Ratios and Proportions

Math topics that you'll learn in this chapter:

✓ Simplifying Ratios

✓ Proportional Ratios

✓ Create Proportion

✓ Similarity and Ratios

23

Topic	Simplifying Ratios
Notes	✓ Ratios are used to make comparisons between two numbers. ✓ Ratios can be written as a fraction, using the word "to", or with a colon. ✓ You can calculate equivalent ratios by multiplying or dividing both sides of the ratio by the same number.
Examples	**Simplify.** $16:56 =$ Both numbers 16 and 56 are divisible by $8 \Rightarrow 16 \div 8 = 2, 56 \div 8 = 7$, Then: $16:56 = 2:7$ **Simplify.** $\frac{35}{45} =$ Both numbers 35 and 45 are divisible by $5, \Rightarrow 35 \div 5 = 7, 45 \div 5 = 9$, Then: $\frac{35}{45} = \frac{7}{9}$

Your Turn!	1) $\frac{5}{45} = -$	2) $\frac{12}{36} = -$
	3) $\frac{15}{60} = -$	4) $\frac{48}{56} = -$
	5) $\frac{24}{96} = -$	6) $\frac{40}{72} = -$
Find more at bit.ly/3nKwq0Z	7) $\frac{24}{80} = -$	8) $\frac{34}{136} = -$

Topic	**Proportional Ratios**
Notes	✓ Two ratios are proportional if they represent the same relationship. ✓ A proportion means that two ratios are equal. It can be written in two ways: $\frac{a}{b} = \frac{c}{d}$ $a : b = c : d$
Example	**Solve this proportion for** x. $\frac{4}{9} = \frac{24}{x}$ Use cross multiplication: $\frac{4}{9} = \frac{24}{x} \Rightarrow 4 \times x = 9 \times 24 \Rightarrow 4x = 216$ Divide to find x: $x = \frac{216}{4} \Rightarrow x = 54$

Your Turn!	1) $\frac{1}{5} = \frac{6}{x} \Rightarrow x = $ ____	2) $\frac{3}{4} = \frac{15}{x} \Rightarrow x = $ ____
	3) $\frac{2}{11} = \frac{4}{x} \Rightarrow x = $ ____	4) $\frac{4}{5} = \frac{x}{20} \Rightarrow x = $ ____
Find more at	5) $\frac{8}{9} = \frac{24}{x} \Rightarrow x = $ ____	6) $\frac{16}{6} = \frac{x}{30} \Rightarrow x = $ ____
bit.ly/37GHQxp	7) $\frac{5}{14} = \frac{30}{x} \Rightarrow x = $ ____	8) $\frac{4}{14} = \frac{34}{x} \Rightarrow x = $ ____

Topic	Create Proportion
Notes	✓ To create a proportion, simply find (or create) two equal fractions. ✓ Use cross products to solve proportions or to test whether two ratios are equal and form a proportion. $\frac{a}{b} = \frac{c}{d} \Rightarrow a \times d = c \times b$
Example	**State if this pair of ratios form a proportion.** $\frac{1}{3}$ **and** $\frac{12}{40}$ Use cross multiplication: $\frac{1}{3} = \frac{12}{40} \rightarrow 1 \times 40 = 12 \times 3 \rightarrow 40 = 36$, which is not correct. Therefore, this pair of ratios doesn't form a proportion.

Your Turn!	**State if each pair of ratios form a proportion.**

1) $\frac{2}{5}$ and $\frac{15}{45}$	2) $\frac{3}{4}$ and $\frac{18}{24}$
3) $\frac{2}{11}$ and $\frac{16}{88}$	4) $\frac{2}{5}$ and $\frac{54}{90}$
5) $\frac{2}{3}$ and $\frac{42}{56}$	6) $\frac{4}{5}$ and $\frac{28}{70}$
7) $\frac{2}{7}$ and $\frac{5}{40}$	8) $\frac{6}{15}$ and $\frac{18}{40}$

Find more at

bit.ly/37GHQxp

9) Solve.

Five pencils costs \$0.60. How many pencils can you buy for \$4.80? _____

Topic	**Similarity and Ratios**
Notes	✓ Two figures are similar if they have the same shape. ✓ Two or more figures are similar if the corresponding angles are equal, and the corresponding sides are in proportion.

Example	**Following triangles are similar. What is the value of unknown side?** **Solution:** Find the corresponding sides and write a proportion: $\frac{4}{12} = \frac{x}{9}$. Now, use cross product to solve for x: $\frac{4}{12} = \frac{x}{9} \rightarrow$ $4 \times 9 = 12 \times x \rightarrow 36 = 12x$. Divide both sides by 12. Then: $12x = 36 \rightarrow \frac{36}{12} = \frac{12x}{12} \rightarrow$ $x = 3$. The missing side is 3.

Your Turn!

1)

?   26   5   13

10   12

2)

35

20   ?

8

3)

14   14   7   7

10   ?   ?

4)

7   14

?   22

Find more at

bit.ly/2KKKmcV

5)

36   9

42   ?

6)

40   ?

20   8

Chapter 4: Answers

Simplifying Ratios

1) $\frac{1}{9}$ 4) $\frac{6}{7}$ 7) $\frac{3}{10}$

2) $\frac{1}{3}$ 5) $\frac{1}{4}$ 8) $\frac{1}{4}$

3) $\frac{1}{4}$ 6) $\frac{5}{9}$

Proportional Ratios

1) 30   4) 16   7) 84

2) 20   5) 27   8) 119

3) 22   6) 80

Create Proportion

1) *No*   4) *No*   7) *No*

2) *Yes*   5) *No*   8) *No*

3) *Yes*   6) *No*   9) 40

Similarity and Ratios

1) 24   3) 5   5) 10.5

2) 14   4) 11   6) 16

CHAPTER

5 Percentage

Math topics that you'll learn in this chapter:

- ✓ Percent Problems
- ✓ Percent of Increase and Decrease
- ✓ Discount, Tax and Tip
- ✓ Simple Interest

29

Topic	Percent Problems

Notes	✓ In each percent problem, we are looking for the base, or part or the percent.
	✓ Use the following equations to find each missing section.
	   ○ Base = Part ÷ Percent
	   ○ Part = Percent × Base
	   ○ Percent = Part ÷ Base

Examples	**12 *is what percent of 40?*** In this problem, we are looking for the percent. Use the following equation: $Percent = Part \div Base \rightarrow Percent = 12 \div 40 = 0.3 = 30\%$ **44 *is 20% of what number?*** Use the following formula: $Base = Part \div Percent \rightarrow$ $Base = 44 \div 0.20 = 220$ 44 is 20% of 220.

Your Turn!		
	1) What is 26 percent of 450?	2) 28 is what percent of 140?
	3) 40 is 5 percent of what number?	4) 32 is what percent of 800?
	5) 82 is 20 percent of what number?	6) 36 is what percent of 720?
Find more at bit.ly/34Gy3FL	7) 66 is 22 percent of what number?	8) 48 is what percent of 800?

Topic	**Percent of Increase and Decrease**
Notes	✓ Percent of change (increase or decrease) is a mathematical concept that represents the degree of change over time. ✓ To find the percentage of increase or decrease: 1- New Number – Original Number 2- The result ÷ Original Number × 100 Or use this formula: $$Percent\ of\ change = \frac{new\ number - original\ number}{original\ number} \times 100$$
Example	The price of a printer increases from \$20 to \$30. What is the percent increase? **Solution:** $Percent\ of\ change = \frac{new\ number - original\ number}{original\ number} \times 100 =$ $\frac{30-20}{20} \times 100 = 50$ The percentage increase is 50. It means that the price of the printer increased 50%
Your Turn! **Find more at** bit.ly/3pgPQes	1) In a class, the number of students has been increased from 24 to 30. What is the percentage increase? _____ %
	2) The price of gasoline rose from \$4.00 to \$4.50 in one month. By what percent did the gas price rise? _____ %
	3) A shirt was originally priced at \$25.00. It went on sale for \$35.00. What was the percent that the shirt was discounted? _____ %
	4) Jason got a raise, and his hourly wage increased from \$20 to \$36. What is the percent increase? _____ %

Topic	Discount, Tax and Tip
Notes	✓ Discount = Multiply the regular price by the rate of discount ✓ Selling price = original price − discount ✓ To find tax, multiply the tax rate to the taxable amount (income, property value, etc.) ✓ To find tip, multiply the rate to the selling price.
Example	The original price of a table is $400 and the tax rate is 5%. What is the final price of the table? **Solution:** First find the tax amount. To find tax: Multiply the tax rate to the taxable amount. Tax rate is 5% or 0.05. Then: $0.05 \times 400 = 20$. The tax amount is $20. Final price is: $400 + $20 = $420

Your Turn!		
	1) Original price of a chair: $360 Tax: 10%, Selling price: _____	2) Original price of a computer: $700 Discount: 20%, Selling price: _____
	3) Original price of a printer: $350 Tax: 10%, Selling price: _____	4) Original price of a sofa: $660 Discount: 45%, Selling price: _____
	5) Original price of a mattress: $840 Tax: 15%, Selling price: _____	6) Original price of a book: $160 Discount: 40%, Selling price: _____
Find more at bit.ly/2Je5lo0 	7) Restaurant bill: $44.00 Tip: 25%, Final amount: _____	8) Restaurant bill: $60.00 Tip: 40%, Final amount: _____

Topic	Simple Interest
Notes	✓ Simple Interest: The charge for borrowing money or the return for lending it. To solve a simple interest problem, use this formula: Interest = principal x rate x time ⇒ $I = p \times r \times t$
Example	***Find simple interest for*** $6,000$ ***investment at*** 2% ***for*** 3 ***years.*** **Solution:** Use Interest formula: $I = prt$ ($p = \$6,000$, $r = 2\% = 0.02$ and $t = 3$) Then: $I = 6,000 \times 0.02 \times 3 = \$360$
Your Turn! **Find more at** bit.ly/3nJli3D	1) $250 at 4% for 3 years. Simple interest: $_____$ 2) $3,400 at 6% for 2 years. Simple interest: $_____$ 3) $780 at 5% for 6 years. Simple interest: $_____$ 4) $3,200 at 9% for 6 years. Simple interest: $_____$ 5) $1,700 at 5% for 3 years. Simple interest: $_____$ 6) $520 at 6% for 5 years. Simple interest: $_____$ 7) $4,300 at 4% for 6 months. Simple interest: $_____$ 8) $800 at 6% for 4 months. Simple interest: $_____$

Chapter 5: Answers

Percent Problems

1) 117
2) 20%
3) 800
4) 4%
5) 410
6) 5%
7) 300
8) 6%

Percent of Increase and Decrease

1) 25%
2) 12.5%
3) 40%
4) 80%

Discount, Tax and Tip

1) $396
2) $560
3) $385
4) $363
5) $966
6) $96
7) $55
8) $84

Simple Interest

1) $30
2) $408
3) $234
4) $1,728
5) $255
6) $156
7) $86
8) $16

CHAPTER

Expressions and Variables

 Math topics that you'll learn in this chapter:

- ✓ Simplifying Variable Expressions
- ✓ Simplifying Polynomial Expressions
- ✓ Evaluating One Variable
- ✓ Evaluating Two Variables
- ✓ The Distributive Property

35

Topic	Simplifying Variable Expressions
Notes	✓ In algebra, a variable is a letter used to stand for a number. The most common letters are: x, y, z, a, b, c, m, and n. ✓ Algebraic expression is an expression contains integers, variables, and the math operations such as addition, subtraction, multiplication, division, etc. ✓ In an expression, we can combine "like" terms. (values with same variable and same power)
Example	*Simplify this expression*. $(7x + 6x + 8) =$? Combine like terms. Then: $(7x + 6x + 8) = 13x + 8$ **(remember you cannot combine variables and numbers).**

Your Turn!		
	1) $8x + 6 - 9x =$	2) $2 + 6x + 4x =$
	3) $3x + 2 - 5x =$	4) $-8 - x^2 - 3x^2 =$
	5) $4 + 11x^2 + 5 =$	6) $7x^2 + 5x + 3x^2 =$
	7) $6x^2 - 11x^2 + 9x =$	8) $6x^2 - 7x - 2x + 3x^2 =$
	9) $5x - (14 - 23x) =$	10) $11x - (54x - 40) =$

Find more at

bit.ly/2WFVudQ

Topic	Simplifying Polynomial Expressions
Notes	✓ In mathematics, a polynomial is an expression consisting of variables and coefficients that involves only the operations of addition, subtraction, multiplication, and non–negative integer exponents of variables. $$P(x) = a_n x^n + a_{n-1} x^{n-1} + \dots + a_2 x^2 + a_1 x + z$$
Example	*Simplify this expression.* $(6x^2 - x^4) - (4x^4 - 2x^2) =$ First use distributive property:→ multiply $(-)$ into $(4x^4 - 2x^2)$ $(6x^2 - x^4) - (4x^4 - 2x^2) = 6x^2 - x^4 - 4x^4 + 2x^2$ Then combine "like" terms: $6x^2 - x^4 - 4x^4 + 2x^2 = 8x^2 - 5x^4$ And write in standard form: $8x^2 - 5x^4 = -5x^4 + 8x^2$

Your Turn!	1) $(x^3 + 5x^2) - (12x + 6x^2) =$	2) $(6x^5 + 3x^3) - (7x^3 + 9x^2) =$
	3) $(10x^4 + 6x^2) - (5x^2 - 7x^4) =$	4) $11x - 9x^2 - 2(3x^2 + 4x^3) =$
	5) $(6x^3 - 2) + 4(3x^2 - 5x^3) =$	6) $(6x^3 - 3x) - 3(2x^3 - 15x^4) =$
Find more at bit.ly/2WT5gtn	7) $7(2x - 3x^3) - 3(x^3 + 6x^2) =$	8) $(8x^2 - 2x) - (7x^3 + 2x^2) =$

Topic	Evaluating One Variable
Notes	✓ To evaluate one variable expression, find the variable and substitute a number for that variable. ✓ Perform the arithmetic operations.
Example	*Find the value of this expression for $x = -5$. $-6x - 16$* **Solution:** Substitute -5 for x, then: $-6x - 16 = -6(-5) - 16 = 30 - 16 = 14$

Your Turn!		
	1) $x = 3 \Rightarrow 5x + 6 =$ _____	2) $x = -4 \Rightarrow 6x - 8 =$ _____
	3) $x = -3 \Rightarrow 7x + 2 =$ _____	4) $x = 5 \Rightarrow 6(4x + 6) =$ _____
	5) $x = 3 \Rightarrow 2(7x - 6) =$ _____	6) $x = 7 \Rightarrow 3(5x + 3) =$ _____
	7) $x = 5 \Rightarrow 8(3x + 10) =$ _____	8) $x = 6 \Rightarrow 4(2x + 9) =$ _____
	9) $x = -8 \Rightarrow -3(x + 5) =$ _____	10) $x = -4 \Rightarrow -2(4x - 6) =$ _____

Find more at

bit.ly/3ppujQZ

Topic	Evaluating Two Variables
Notes	✓ To evaluate an algebraic expression, substitute a number for each variable. ✓ Perform the arithmetic operations to find the value of the expression.
Example	*Evaluate this expression for* $a = 8$ *and* $b = -3$. $2a - 3b$ **Solution:** Substitute 8 for a, and -3 for b, then: $2a - 3b = 2(8) - 3(-3) = 16 + 9 = 25$

Your Turn!		
	1) $-2a + 4b$, $a = 4$, $b = 2$ _____	2) $5x + 3y$, $x = -6$, $y = 3$ _____
	3) $-3a + 4b$, $a = 3$, $b = -4$ _____	4) $6x - 3y$, $x = 2$, $y = -2$ _____
	5) $3z + 11 + 4k$, $z = 5$, $k = 2$ _____	6) $6a - (8 - 4b)$, $a = 2$, $b = 3$ _____
	7) $-4a + 2b$, $a = 6$, $b = 4$ _____	8) $-3a + b$, $a = -5$, $b = 8$ _____
	9) $6x + 2y$, $x = -3$, $y = 7$ _____	10) $-z + 2 + 4k$, $z = -5$, $k = -4$ _____

Find more at

bit.ly/2JfrzWJ

Topic	The Distributive Property
Notes	✓ The distributive property (or the distributive property of multiplication over addition and subtraction) simplifies and solves expressions in the form of: $a(b + c)$ or $a(b - c)$ ✓ Distributive Property rule: $$a(b + c) = ab + ac$$
Example	***Simply.*** $(4)(3x - 7)$ **Solution:** Use Distributive Property rule: $a(b + c) = ab + ac$ $(4)(3x - 7) = (4 \times 3x) + (4) \times (-7) = 12x - 28$

Your Turn!

1) $(-2)(5 - 6x) =$	2) $(4 - 3x)(-4)$
3) $7(3 - 6x) =$	4) $15(2 - x) =$
5) $6(4 - 2x) =$	6) $(-3)(-4x + 2) =$
7) $(7 - 3x)(4) =$	8) $(-15x + 11)(-4) =$
9) $(-9x + 3)(-2) =$	10) $(-10x + 22)(-4) =$

Find more at

bit.ly/38qCaXs

Chapter 6: Answers

Simplifying Variable Expressions

1) $-x + 6$
2) $10x + 2$
3) $-2x + 2$
4) $-4x^2 - 8$

5) $11x^2 + 9$
6) $10x^2 + 5x$
7) $-5x^2 + 9x$
8) $9x^2 - 9x$

9) $28x - 14$
10) $-43x + 40$

Simplifying Polynomial Expressions

1) $x^3 - x^2 - 12x$
2) $6x^5 - 4x^3 - 9x^2$
3) $17x^4 + x^2$
4) $-8x^3 - 15x^2 + 11x$

5) $-14x^3 + 12x^2 - 2$
6) $45x^4 - 3x$
7) $-24x^3 - 18x^2 + 14x$
8) $-7x^3 - 6x^2 - 2x$

Evaluating One Variable

1) 21
2) -32
3) -19
4) 156

5) 30
6) 114
7) 200
8) 84

9) 9
10) 44

Evaluating Two Variables

1) 0
2) -21
3) -25
4) 18

5) 34
6) 16
7) -16
8) 23

9) -4
10) -9

The Distributive Property

1) $12x - 10$
2) $12x - 16$
3) $-42x + 21$
4) $-15x + 30$

5) $-12x + 24$
6) $12x - 6$
7) $-12x + 28$
8) $60x - 44$

9) $18x - 6$
10) $40x - 88$

CHAPTER

7 **Equations and Inequalities**

Math topics that you'll learn in this chapter:

- ✓ One-Step Equations
- ✓ Multi-Step Equations
- ✓ System of Equations
- ✓ Graphing Single–Variable Inequalities
- ✓ One-Step Inequalities
- ✓ Multi-Step Inequalities

43

Topic	One–Step Equations

Notes	✓ You only need to perform one Math operation in order to solve the one-step equations.
	✓ To solve one-step equation, find the inverse (opposite) operation is being performed.
	✓ The inverse operations are:
	   - Addition and subtraction
	   - Multiplication and division

Example	***Solve this equation.*** $x + 48 = 63 \Rightarrow x = ?$ Here, the operation is addition and its inverse operation is subtraction. To solve this equation, subtract 48 from both sides of the equation: $x + 48 - 48 = 63 - 48$ Then simplify: $x + 48 - 48 = 63 - 48 \Rightarrow x = 15$

Your Turn!	1) $x - 14 = 54 \Rightarrow x =$ ____	2) $18 = 12 + x \Rightarrow x =$ ____
	3) $x - 24 = 58 \Rightarrow x =$ ____	4) $x + 16 = 29 \Rightarrow x =$ ____
	5) $6x = 30 \Rightarrow x =$ ____	6) $\frac{x}{5} = -9 \Rightarrow x =$ ____
Find more at bit.ly/37Jq0tK	7) $12x = 96 \Rightarrow x =$ ____	8) $\frac{x}{16} = -3 \Rightarrow x =$ ____

Topic	Multi –Step Equations
Notes	✓ Combine "like" terms on one side. ✓ Bring variables to one side by adding or subtracting. ✓ Simplify using the inverse of addition or subtraction. ✓ Simplify further by using the inverse of multiplication or division. ✓ Check your solution by plugging the value of the variable into the original equation.
Example	**Solve this equation for** x. $3x - 4 = 17$ **Solution:** The inverse of subtraction is addition. Add 4 to both sides of the equation. Then: $3x - 4 = 17 \Rightarrow 3x - 4 = 17 + 4$ $\Rightarrow 3x = 21$. Now, divide both sides by 3, then: $\frac{3x}{3} = \frac{21}{3} \Rightarrow x = 7$ Now, check the solution: $x = 7 \Rightarrow 3x - 4 = 17 \Rightarrow 3(7) - 4 = 17 \Rightarrow$ $21 - 4 = 17$ The answer $x = 7$ is correct.

Your Turn!	1) $6x - 18 = 12 \Rightarrow x =$	2) $16 - 4x = -5 + 3x \Rightarrow x =$
	3) $2(2 - 3x) = 28 \Rightarrow x =$	4) $14 + 2x = -6 - 8x \Rightarrow x =$
	5) $-4(6 + x) = 8 \Rightarrow x =$	6) $14 - 3x = -2 - 7x \Rightarrow x =$
Find more at bit.ly/3nQbSEB	7) $16 = -(x - 7) \Rightarrow x =$	8) $14 - 6x = -4 - 3x \Rightarrow x =$

Topic	System of Equations
Notes	✓ A system of equations contains two equations and two variables. For example, consider the system of equations: $x - 2y = -2, x + 2y = 10$ ✓ The easiest way to solve a system of equation is using the elimination method. The elimination method uses the addition property of equality. You can add the same value to each side of an equation. ✓ For the first equation above, you can add $x + 2y$ to the left side and 10 to the right side of the first equation: $x - 2y + (x + 2y) = -2 + 10$. Now, if you simplify, you get: $x - 2y + (x + 2y) = -2 + 10 \rightarrow 2x = 8 \rightarrow x = 4$. Now, substitute 4 for the x in the first equation: $4 - 2y = -2$. By solving this equation, $y = 3$
Example	What is the value of x and y in this system of equations? $\begin{cases} 4x - y = 18 \\ -x + 4y = 3 \end{cases}$ **Solution:** Solving System of Equations by Elimination: $\begin{array}{r} 4x - y = 18 \\ -x + 4y = 3 \\ \hline \end{array}$ Multiply the second equation by 4, then add it to the first equation. $\begin{array}{l} 4x - y = 18 \\ 4(-x + 4y = 3) \end{array} \Rightarrow \begin{array}{r} 4x - y = 18 \\ -4x + 16y = 12 \\ \hline \end{array} \Rightarrow 15y = 30 \Rightarrow y = 2$. Now, substitute 2 for y in the first equation and solve for x. $4x - (2) = 18 \Rightarrow 4x = 20 \Rightarrow x = 5$

Your Turn!
 	
 Find more at
 	
 bit.ly/3mPGO6k
	1) $3x - y = 7$
	     $2x + y = 13$
	
	     $x = $ ___
	     $y = $ ___
	
	 3) $x + y = -5$
	     $3x + 2y = 12$
	
	     $x = $ ___
	     $y = $ ___
	
	 5) $7x + y = 50$
	     $14x - 2y = -44$
	
	     $x = $ ___
	     $y = $ ___
		2) $4x + 8y = -24$
		     $-4x - 2y = -12$
		
		     $x = $ ___
		     $y = $ ___
		
		 4) $y = x - 1$
		     $y = 2x - 3$
		
		     $x = $ ___
		     $y = $ ___
		
		 6) $4x + 2y = 14$
		     $7x - 3y = -8$
		
		     $x = $ ___
		     $y = $ ___

Topic	**Graphing Single–Variable Inequalities**
Notes	✓ An inequality compares two expressions using an inequality sign. ✓ Inequality signs are: "less than" $<$, "greater than" $>$, "less than or equal to" $\leq$, and "greater than or equal to" $\geq$. ✓ To graph a single–variable inequality, find the value of the inequality on the number line. ✓ For less than ($<$) or greater than ($>$) draw open circle on the value of the variable. If there is an equal sign too, then use filled circle. ✓ Draw an arrow to the right for greater or to the left for less than.
Example	***Draw a graph for this inequality.*** $x < 4$ **Solution:** Since, the variable is less than 4, then we need to find 4 in the number line and draw an open circle on it. Then, draw an arrow to the left. -6 -5 -4 -3 -2 -1 0 1 2 3 4 5 6

Your Turn!	1) $x < 1$ -6 -5 -4 -3 -2 -1 0 1 2 3 4 5 6	2) $x \geq -5$ -6 -5 -4 -3 -2 -1 0 1 2 3 4 5 6
	3) $x \geq -4$ -6 -5 -4 -3 -2 -1 0 1 2 3 4 5 6	4) $x \leq 6$ -6 -5 -4 -3 -2 -1 0 1 2 3 4 5 6
	5) $x > -6$ -6 -5 -4 -3 -2 -1 0 1 2 3 4 5 6	6) $5 > x$ -6 -5 -4 -3 -2 -1 0 1 2 3 4 5 6
Find more at bit.ly/3aJ4GGo	7) $-2 \leq x$ -6 -5 -4 -3 -2 -1 0 1 2 3 4 5 6	8) $x > 3$ -6 -5 -4 -3 -2 -1 0 1 2 3 4 5 6

Topic	One–Step Inequalities
Notes	✓ Inequality signs are: "less than" $<$, "greater than" $>$, "less than or equal to" $\leq$, and "greater than or equal to" $\geq$. ✓ You only need to perform one Math operation in order to solve the one-step inequalities. ✓ To solve one-step inequalities, find the inverse (opposite) operation is being performed. ✓ For dividing or multiplying both sides by negative numbers, flip the direction of the inequality sign.
Example	**Solve this inequality.** $x + 18 < 56 \Rightarrow$ _____ Here, the operation is addition and its inverse operation is subtraction. To solve this inequality, subtract 18 from both sides of the inequality: $x + 18 - 18 < 56 - 18$ Then simplify: $x < 38$

Your Turn!

1) $4x < -8 \Rightarrow$ _____

2) $x - 9 > 32 \Rightarrow$ _____

3) $-4x \geq 48 \Rightarrow$ _____

4) $x - 12 \leq 8 \Rightarrow$ _____

5) $\frac{x}{5} \geq -7 \Rightarrow$ _____

6) $54 < 6x \Rightarrow$ _____

Find more at

bit.ly/3rrElgL

7) $84 \leq 12x \Rightarrow$ _____

8) $\frac{x}{9} > -9 \Rightarrow$ _____

Topic	Multi − Step Inequalities
Notes	✓ Isolate the variable. ✓ Simplify using the inverse of addition or subtraction. ✓ Simplify further by using the inverse of multiplication or division. ✓ For dividing or multiplying both sides by negative numbers, flip the direction of the inequality sign.
Example	***Solve this inequality.*** $4x + 10 \leq 26$ **Solution:** First subtract 10 from both sides: $4x + 10 - 10 \leq 26 - 10$ Then simplify: $4x + 10 - 10 \leq 26 - 10 \rightarrow 4x \leq 16$ Now divide both sides by 4: $\frac{4x}{4} \leq \frac{16}{4} \rightarrow x \leq 4$

Your Turn!

1) $2x + 6 < 30 \rightarrow$ _____	2) $4x - 8 \leq 12 \rightarrow$ _____
3) $6x - 2 \leq 22 \rightarrow$ _____	4) $18 - 5x \geq -7 \rightarrow$ _____
5) $22 - 4x \geq -10 \rightarrow$ _____	6) $6x - 10 \leq 20 \rightarrow$ _____
7) $8 + 9x < 62 \rightarrow$ _____	8) $8 - 9x < 89 \rightarrow$ _____

Find more at

bit.ly/2WK1xOr

Chapter 7: Answers

One-Step Equations

1) 68

2) 6

3) 82

4) 13

5) 5

6) −45

7) 8

8) −48

Multi-Step Equations

1) 5

2) 3

3) −4

4) −2

5) −8

6) −4

7) −9

8) 6

System of Equations

1) $x = 4, y = 5$

2) $x = 6, y = -6$

3) $x = 22, y = -27$

4) $x = 2, y = 1$

5) $x = 2, y = 36$

6) $x = 1, y = 5$

Graphing Single-Variable Inequalities

1)

2)

3)

4)

5)

6)

7)

8)

One-Step Inequalities

1) $x < -2$

2) $x > 41$

3) $x \leq -12$

4) $x \leq 20$

5) $x \geq -35$

6) $9 < x$

7) $7 \leq x$

8) $x > -81$

Multi-Step Inequalities

1) $x < 12$

2) $x \leq 5$

3) $x \leq 4$

4) $x \leq 5$

5) $x \leq 8$

6) $x \leq 5$

7) $x < 6$

8) $x > -9$

CHAPTER

8 **Lines and Slope**

Math topics that you'll learn in this chapter:

- ✓ Finding Slope
- ✓ Graphing Lines Using Slope–Intercept Form
- ✓ Writing Linear Equations
- ✓ Finding Midpoint
- ✓ Finding Distance of Two Points

53

Topic	Finding Slope
Notes	✓ The slope of a line represents the direction of a line on the coordinate plane. ✓ A line on coordinate plane can be drawn by connecting two points. ✓ To find the slope of a line, we need two points. ✓ The slope of a line with two points A (x_1, y_1) and B (x_2, y_2) can be found by using this formula: $\frac{y_2-y_1}{x_2-x_1} = \frac{rise}{run}$ ✓ The equation of a line is typically written as $y = mx + b$ where m is the slope and b is the y-intercept.
Examples	***Find the slope of the line through these two points:*** $(5, -10)$ ***and*** $(9, 6)$. **Solution:** Slope $= \frac{y_2-y_1}{x_2-x_1}$. Let (x_1, y_1) be $(5, -10)$ and (x_2, y_2) be $(9, 6)$. Then: slope $= \frac{y_2-y_1}{x_2-x_1} = \frac{6-(-10)}{9-5} = \frac{6+10}{4} = \frac{16}{4} = 4$ ***Find the slope of the line with equation*** $y = 3x - 7$ **Solution:** when the equation of a line is written in the form of $y = mx + b$, the slope is m. In this line: $y = 3x - 7$, the slope is 3.

Your Turn!	1) $(1, 2), (6, 7)$ Slope = ____	2) $(-4, 2), (0, 6)$ Slope = ____
	3) $(-3, -1), (-4, 2)$ Slope = ____	4) $(-5, 3), (5, -1)$ Slope = ____
Find more at bit.ly/3nMJYJv	5) $y = 2x + 11$ Slope = ____	6) $y = -5x + 9$ Slope = ____

Topic	Graphing Lines Using Slope–Intercept Form
Notes	✓ Slope–intercept form of a line: given the slope m and the y–intercept (the intersection of the line and y –axis) b, then the equation of the line is: $$y = mx + b$$

Example	***Sketch the graph of*** $y = -3x - 2$. **Solution:** To graph this line, we need to find two points. When x is zero the value of y is -2. And when y is zero the value of x is $-\frac{2}{3}$. $$x = 0 \rightarrow y = -3(0) - 2 = -2, y = 0 \rightarrow 0$$ $$= -3x - 2 \rightarrow x = -\frac{2}{3}$$ Now, we have two points: $(0, -3)$ and $(-\frac{2}{3}, 0)$. Find the points and graph the line. Remember that the slope of the line is $-\frac{2}{3}$.

Your Turn!	1) $y = -2x + 1$	2) $y = -x - 6$
Find more at bit.ly/3hfdnJL		

Topic	Writing Linear Equations
Notes	✓ The equation of a line: $y = mx + b$ ✓ Identify the slope. ✓ Find the y–intercept. This can be done by substituting the slope and the coordinates of a point (x, y) on the line.
Example	**Write the equation of the line through $(2, 1)$ and $(-1, 7)$.** **Solution:** Slope $= \frac{y_2 - y_1}{x_2 - x_1} = \frac{7-1}{-1-2} = \frac{6}{-3} = -2 \rightarrow m = -2$ To find the value of b, you can use either points. The answer will be the same: $y = -2x + b$ $(2, 1) \rightarrow 1 = -2(2) + b \rightarrow b = 5$ $(-1, 7) \rightarrow 7 = -2(-1) + b \rightarrow b = 5$ The equation of the line is: $y = -2x + 5$

Your Turn!	1) through: $(-1, 2), (1, 8)$ $y =$	2) through: $(7, 1), (5, 9)$ $y =$
	3) through: $(3, -3), (8, 2)$ $y =$	4) through: $(-2, 2), (4, -10)$ $y =$
	5) through: $(4, -6), (-5, 12)$ $y =$	6) through: $(3, -3), (-2, 7)$ $y =$
Find more at bit.ly/3nMKcAl	7) through $(-2, 4)$, Slope: 3 $y =$	8) through $(5, -2)$, Slope: -6 $y =$

Topic	Finding Midpoint
Notes	✓ The middle of a line segment is its midpoint. ✓ The Midpoint of two endpoints A (x_1, y_1) and B (x_2, y_2) can be found using this formula: $M\left(\frac{x_1+x_2}{2}, \frac{y_1+y_2}{2}\right)$
Example	Find the midpoint of the line segment with the given endpoints. $(2, -2), (4, 8)$ **Solution:** Midpoint $= \left(\frac{x_1+x_2}{2}, \frac{y_1+y_2}{2}\right) \rightarrow (x_1, y_1) = (2, -2)$ and $(x_2, y_2) = (4, 8)$ Midpoint $= \left(\frac{2+4}{2}, \frac{-2+8}{2}\right) \rightarrow \left(\frac{6}{2}, \frac{6}{2}\right) \rightarrow M(3, 3)$

Your Turn!	1) $(3, 2), (-7, 2)$ **Midpoint** = (___, ___)	2) $(4, 1), (10, 5)$ **Midpoint** = (___, ___)
	3) $(-3, 3), (5, 3)$ **Midpoint** = (___, ___)	4) $(8, 3), (-4, 5)$ **Midpoint** = (___, ___)
	5) $(5, 4), (-1, 2)$ **Midpoint** = (___, ___)	6) $(6, -4), (6, 6)$ **Midpoint** = (___, ___)
Find more at bit.ly/3nPdnTq	7) $(9, 4), (-1, -6)$ **Midpoint** = (___, ___)	8) $(7, 4), (-1, 10)$ **Midpoint** = (___, ___)
	9) $(-2, 7), (4, -5)$ **Midpoint** = (___, ___)	10) $(-16, -3), (2, -5)$ **Midpoint** = (___, ___)

Topic	Finding Distance of Two Points
Notes	✓ Use this formula to find the distance of two points A (x_1, y_1) and B (x_2, y_2): $$d = \sqrt{(x_2 - x_1)^2 + (y_2 - y_1)^2}$$
Example	***Find the distance of two points*** $(8, 2)$ ***and*** $(-6, 2)$. **Solution:** ***Use distance of two points formula:*** $d = \sqrt{(x_2 - x_1)^2 + (y_2 - y_1)^2}$ $(x_1, y_1) = (8, 2)$, and $(x_2, y_2) = (-6, 2)$ Then: $d = \sqrt{(x_2 - x_1)^2 + (y_2 - y_1)^2} \rightarrow d = \sqrt{(-6 - (8))^2 + (2 - 2)^2} = \sqrt{(14)^2 + (0)^2} = \sqrt{196 + 0} = \sqrt{196} = 14$

Your Turn!	1) $(0, 0), (6, 8)$
	
	    Distance = ____ 2) $(-6, 12), (-6, 10)$
	
	                                       Distance = ____

1) $(0, 0), (6, 8)$

   Distance = ____

2) $(-6, 12), (-6, 10)$

   Distance = ____

3) $(9, 4), (-5, 4)$

   Distance = ____

4) $(8, 9), (3, -3)$

   Distance = ____

5) $(-5, 24), (-5, 20)$

   Distance = ____

6) $(-2, 5), (4, -3)$

   Distance = ____

Find more at

bit.ly/2KV50Hy

7) $(4, 4), (7, 8)$

   Distance = ____

8) $(4, -1), (14, 23)$

   Distance = ____

Chapter 8: Answers

Finding Slope

1) 1

2) 1

3) -3

4) $-\dfrac{2}{5}$

5) 2

6) -5

Graphing Lines Using Slope-Intercept Form

1)

2)

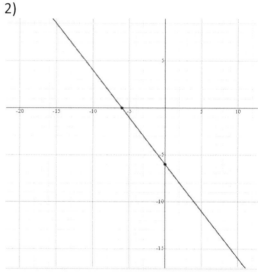

Writing Linear Equations

1) $y = 3x + 5$

2) $y = -4x + 29$

3) $y = x - 6$

4) $y = -2x - 2$

5) $y = -2x + 2$

6) $y = -2x + 3$

7) $y = 3x + 10$

8) $y = -6x + 28$

Finding Midpoint

1) $(-2, 2)$

2) $(7, 3)$

3) $(1, 3)$

4) $(2, 4)$

5) $(2, 3)$

6) $(6, 1)$

7) $(4, -1)$

8) $(3, 7)$

9) $(1, 1)$

10) $(-7, -4)$

Finding Distance of Two points

1) 10

2) 2

3) 14

4) 13

5) 4

6) 10

7) 5

8) 26

CHAPTER

9 Exponents and Variables

Math topics that you'll learn in this chapter:

- ✓ Multiplication Property of Exponents
- ✓ Division Property of Exponents
- ✓ Powers of Products and Quotients
- ✓ Zero and Negative Exponents
- ✓ Negative Exponents and Negative Bases
- ✓ Scientific Notation
- ✓ Radicals

61

Topic	**Multiplication Property of Exponents**
Notes	✓ Exponents are shorthand for repeated multiplication of the same number by itself. For example, instead of 2×2, we can write 2^2. For $3 \times 3 \times 3 \times 3$, we can write 3^4 ✓ In algebra, a variable is a letter used to stand for a number. The most common letters are: $x, y, z, a, b, c, m,$ and n. ✓ Exponent's rules: $x^a \times x^b = x^{a+b}$, $\dfrac{x^a}{x^b} = x^{a-b}$ $\quad\quad (x^a)^b = x^{a \times b} \quad\quad\quad (xy)^a = x^a \times y^a \quad\quad \left(\dfrac{a}{b}\right)^c = \dfrac{a^c}{b^c}$
Example	**Multiply.** $6x^5 \times 4x^2$ Use Exponent's rules: $x^a \times x^b = x^{a+b} \rightarrow x^5 \times x^2 = x^{5+2} = x^7$ Then: $6x^5 \times 4x^2 = 24x^7$

Your Turn!		
	1) $x^3 \times 4x =$	2) $5x^4 \times x^3 =$
	3) $5x^3 \times 2x^4 =$	4) $7x^2 \times 9xy =$
	5) $4x^7 y \times 3x^2 y^4 =$	6) $5x^3 y^2 \times 6x^2 y^6 =$
	7) $9x^2 y \times 3x^5 y^6 =$	8) $8x^6 \times 4x^8 y^4 =$
Find more at bit.ly/34AWHr1	9) $8x^3 y^7 \times 5x^5 y^2 =$	10) $2x^7 y^3 \times 9xy^2 =$

Topic	**Division Property of Exponents**
Notes	✓ For division of exponents use these formulas: $\frac{x^a}{x^b} = x^{a-b}$, $x \neq 0$ $\frac{x^a}{x^b} = \frac{1}{x^{b-a}}$, $x \neq 0$, $\qquad \frac{1}{x^b} = x^{-b}$
Example	***Simplify.*** $\frac{4x^4 y}{36x^2 y^2}$ First cancel the common factor: $4 \rightarrow \frac{4x^4 y}{36x^2 y^2} = \frac{x^4 y}{9x^2 y^2}$ Use Exponent's rules: $\frac{x^a}{x^b} = x^{a-b} \rightarrow \frac{x^4}{x^2} = x^{4-2} = x^2$ Then: $\frac{4x^4 y}{36x^2 y^2} = \frac{xy}{9y^2} \rightarrow$ now cancel the common factor: $y \rightarrow \frac{xy}{9y^2} = \frac{x}{9y}$

Your Turn!	1) $\dfrac{3^6}{3^2} =$	2) $\dfrac{5x}{15x^4} =$
	3) $\dfrac{6x^2}{2x^5} =$	4) $\dfrac{14x^3}{21x^7} =$
	5) $\dfrac{12x^4}{18y^5} =$	6) $\dfrac{28xy^4}{7x^5 y^3} =$
	7) $\dfrac{2x^3 y^8}{5xy^2} =$	8) $\dfrac{4x^3 y^7}{10x^4} =$
Find more at bit.ly/37JAclZ	9) $\dfrac{6x^3}{24x^7 y^5} =$	10) $\dfrac{16y^6 x^4}{32y^2 x^9} =$

Topic	Powers of Products and Quotients
Notes	✓ For any nonzero numbers a and b and any integer x, $$(ab)^x = a^x \times b^x, \left(\frac{a}{b}\right)^c = \frac{a^c}{b^c}$$
Example	**Simplify.** $\left(\frac{3x^4}{x}\right)^2$ First cancel the common factor: $x \rightarrow \left(\frac{3x^4}{x}\right)^2 = (3x^3)^2$ Use Exponent's rules: $(ab)^x = a^x \times b^x$ Then: $(3x^3)^2 = (3)^2(x^3)^2 = 9x^6$

Your Turn!		
	1) $(2x^3x^2)^3 =$	2) $(3x^4 \times 4x)^2 =$
	3) $(9x^{10}y^3)^2 =$	4) $(8x^7y^3)^2 =$
	5) $(6x^5y^6)^3 =$	6) $(2x \times 4y^6)^2 =$
	7) $\left(\frac{9x}{x^3}\right)^2 =$	8) $\left(\frac{x^5y^6}{x^2y^2}\right)^3 =$
	9) $\left(\frac{28x}{4x^7}\right)^2 =$	10) $\left(\frac{32x^6}{40x^4y^3}\right)^2 =$

Find more at

bit.ly/34CgPJm

Topic	Zero and Negative Exponents
Notes	✓ A negative exponent is the reciprocal of that number with a positive exponent. $(3)^{-2} = \frac{1}{3^2}$ ✓ Zero-Exponent Rule: $a^0 = 1$, this means that anything raised to the zero power is 1. For example: $(28x^2y)^0 = 1$
Example	*Evaluate.* $\left(\frac{1}{4}\right)^{-2} =$ Use negative exponent's rule: $\left(\frac{1}{x^a}\right)^{-2} = (x^a)^2 \rightarrow \left(\frac{1}{4}\right)^{-2} = (4)^2 =$ Then: $(4)^2 = 16$

Your Turn!	1) $2^{-5} =$	2) $3^{-3} =$
	3) $5^{-3} =$	4) $1^{-7} =$
	5) $6^{-3} =$	6) $4^{-3} =$
	7) $10^{-4} =$	8) $7^{-3} =$
Find more at bit.ly/3rnkh4v	9) $\left(\frac{1}{9}\right)^{-1} =$	10) $\left(\frac{1}{7}\right)^{-4} =$

Topic	Negative Exponents and Negative Bases
Notes	✓ Make the power positive. A negative exponent is the reciprocal of that number with a positive exponent. ✓ The parenthesis is important! 5^{-2} is not the same as $(-5)^{-2}$ $$(-5)^{-2} = -\frac{1}{5^2} \text{ and } (-5)^{-2} = +\frac{1}{5^2}$$
Example	*Simplify.* $\left(-\dfrac{5x}{6yz}\right)^{-3} =$ Use negative exponent's rule: $\left(\dfrac{x^a}{x^b}\right)^{-2} = \left(\dfrac{x^b}{x^a}\right)^2 \rightarrow \left(-\dfrac{5x}{6yz}\right)^{-3} = \left(-\dfrac{6yz}{5x}\right)^3$ Now use exponent's rule: $\left(\dfrac{a}{b}\right)^c = \dfrac{a^c}{b^c} \rightarrow \left(-\dfrac{6yz}{5x}\right)^3 = -\dfrac{6^3 y^3 z^3}{5^3 x^3} = -\dfrac{216 y^3 z^3}{125 x^3}$

Your Turn!		
	1) $-3x^{-4}y^{-2} =$	2) $20x^{-7}y^{-2} =$
	3) $18a^{-9}b^{-8} =$	4) $-10x^3 y^{-4} =$
	5) $-\dfrac{27}{x^{-6}} =$	6) $\dfrac{8b}{-9c^{-5}} =$
	7) $\dfrac{10ab}{a^{-4}b^{-2}} =$	8) $-\dfrac{6n^{-2}}{18p^{-4}} =$
	9) $\dfrac{48ab^{-1}}{-3c^{-4}} =$	10) $\left(\dfrac{9a}{6c}\right)^{-3} =$

Find more at

bit.ly/3nPROSM

Topic	Scientific Notation
Notes	✓ It is used to write very big or very small numbers in decimal form. ✓ In scientific notation all numbers are written in the form of: $$m \times 10^n$$ | Decimal notation	Scientific notation | |---|---| | 3 | 3×10^0 | | $-45,000$ | -4.5×10^4 | | 0.3 | 3×10^{-1} | | 2,122.456 | 2.122456×10^3 |

Example	**Write 0.00049 in scientific notation.** First, move the decimal point to the right so that you have a number that is between 1 and 10. Then: $m = 4.9$ Now, determine how many places the decimal moved in step 1 by the power of 10. Then: $10^{-4} \rightarrow$ When the decimal moved to the right, the exponent is negative. Then: $0.00049 = 4.9 \times 10^{-4}$

Your Turn!		
	1) $0.000281 =$	2) $0.00056 =$
	3) $37,000,000 =$	4) $19,000 =$
	5) $4 \times 10^{-1} =$	6) $8 \times 10^{-2} =$
Find more at bit.ly/3nOwJYP	7) $2.6 \times 10^4 =$	8) $7.2 \times 10^{-5} =$

Topic	Radicals
Notes	✓ If n is a positive integer and x is a real number, then: $\sqrt[n]{x} = x^{\frac{1}{n}}$, $$\sqrt[n]{xy} = x^{\frac{1}{n}} \times y^{\frac{1}{n}}, \sqrt[n]{\frac{x}{y}} = \frac{x^{\frac{1}{n}}}{y^{\frac{1}{n}}}, \text{ and } \sqrt[n]{x} \times \sqrt[n]{y} = \sqrt[n]{xy}$$ ✓ A square root of x is a number r whose square is: $r^2 = x$ (r is a square root of x. ✓ To add and subtract radicals, we need to have the same values under the radical. For example: $\sqrt{3} + \sqrt{3} = 2\sqrt{3}$, $3\sqrt{5} - \sqrt{5} = 2\sqrt{5}$
Example	*Evaluate.* $\sqrt{18} + \sqrt{8} =$ **Solution:** Since we do not have the same values under the radical, we cannot add these two radicals. But we can simplify each radical. $$\sqrt{18} = \sqrt{9} \times \sqrt{2} = 3\sqrt{2} \text{ and } \sqrt{8} = \sqrt{4} \times \sqrt{2} = 2\sqrt{2}$$ Now, we have the same values under the radical. Then: $$\sqrt{18} + \sqrt{8} = 3\sqrt{2} + 2\sqrt{2} = 5\sqrt{2}$$
Your Turn! **Find more at** bit.ly/2WEATqr	1) $\sqrt{5} \times \sqrt{5} =$ 2) $\sqrt{8} \times \sqrt{2} =$ 3) $\sqrt{3} \times \sqrt{12} =$ 4) $\sqrt{48} \div \sqrt{3} =$ 5) $\sqrt{2} + \sqrt{18} =$ 6) $\sqrt{28} - \sqrt{7} =$ 7) $4\sqrt{5} - 2\sqrt{5} =$ 8) $7\sqrt{7} \times 3\sqrt{7} =$

Chapter 9: Answers

Multiplication Property of Exponents

1) $4x^4$

2) $5x^7$

3) $10x^7$

4) $63x^3y$

5) $12x^9y^5$

6) $30x^5y^8$

7) $27x^7y^7$

8) $32x^{14}y^4$

9) $40x^8y^9$

10) $18x^8y^5$

Division Property of Exponents

1) 3^4

2) $\dfrac{1}{3x^3}$

3) $\dfrac{3}{x^3}$

4) $\dfrac{2}{3x^4}$

5) $\dfrac{2x^4}{3y^5}$

6) $\dfrac{4y}{x^4}$

7) $\dfrac{2x^2y^6}{5}$

8) $\dfrac{2y^7}{5x}$

9) $\dfrac{1}{4x^4y^5}$

10) $\dfrac{y^4}{2x^5}$

Powers of Products and Quotients

1) $8x^{15}$

2) $144x^{10}$

3) $81x^{20}y^6$

4) $64x^{14}y^6$

5) $216x^{15}y^{18}$

6) $64x^2y^{12}$

7) $\dfrac{81}{x^4}$

8) x^9y^{12}

9) $\dfrac{49}{x^{12}}$

10) $\dfrac{16x^4}{25y^6}$

Zero and Negative Exponents

1) $\dfrac{1}{32}$

2) $\dfrac{1}{27}$

3) $\dfrac{1}{125}$

4) 1

5) $\dfrac{1}{216}$

6) $\dfrac{1}{64}$

7) $\dfrac{1}{10,000}$

8) $\dfrac{1}{343}$

9) 9

10) $2,401$

Negative Exponents and Negative Bases

1) $-\dfrac{3}{x^4 y^2}$

2) $\dfrac{20}{x^7 y^2}$

3) $\dfrac{18}{a^9 b^8}$

4) $-\dfrac{10x^3}{y^4}$

5) $-27x^6$

6) $-\dfrac{8bc^5}{9}$

7) $10a^5 b^3$

8) $-\dfrac{p^4}{3n^2}$

9) $-\dfrac{16ac^4}{b}$

10) $\dfrac{8c^3}{27a^3}$

Scientific Notation

1) 2.81×10^{-4}

2) 5.6×10^{-4}

3) 3.7×10^7

4) 1.9×10^4

5) 0.4

6) 0.08

7) $26,000$

8) 0.000072

Radicals

1) 5

2) 4

3) 6

4) 4

5) $4\sqrt{2}$

6) $\sqrt{7}$

7) $2\sqrt{5}$

8) 147

CHAPTER

10 Polynomials

Math topics that you'll learn in this chapter:

- ✓ Simplifying Polynomials
- ✓ Adding and Subtracting Polynomials
- ✓ Multiplying Binomials
- ✓ Multiplying and Dividing Monomials
- ✓ Multiplying a Polynomial and a Monomial
- ✓ Multiplying Monomials
- ✓ Factoring Trinomials

71

Topic	Simplifying Polynomials
Notes	✓ Find "like" terms. (they have same variables with same power). ✓ Use "FOIL". (First–Out–In–Last) for binomials: $$(x + a)(x + b) = x^2 + (b + a)x + ab$$ ✓ Add or Subtract "like" terms using order of operation.
Example	**Simplify this expression.** $(x + 2)(x - 5) =$ **Solution:** First apply FOIL method: $(a + b)(c + d) = ac + ad + bc + bd$ $(x + 2)(x - 5) = x^2 - 5x + 2x - 10$ Now combine like terms: $x^2 - 5x + 2x - 10 = x^2 - 3x - 10$
Your Turn!	1) $-(5x - 2) =$ _____ 2) $2(4x + 9) =$ _____ 3) $4x(2x - 5) =$ _____ 4) $6x(2x + 7) =$ _____ 5) $-3x(4x + 2) + 6x =$ _____ 6) $-5x(9x - 2) - 2x^2 =$ _____ 7) $(x + 1)(x + 5) =$ _____ 8) $(x + 6)(x + 8) =$ _____ 9) $-3x^2 + 8x^3 + 12x^2 =$ _____ 10) $-7x^5 + 9x^4 + 4x^5 =$ _____

Find more at

bit.ly/3rnAcj8

Topic	Adding and Subtracting Polynomials
Notes	✓ Adding polynomials is just a matter of combining like terms, with some order of operations considerations thrown in. ✓ Be careful with the minus signs, and don't confuse addition and multiplication!
Example	**Simplify the expressions.** $(5x^2 - 2x^3) - (4x^3 - 8x^2) =$ **Solution:** First use Distributive Property: $-(4x^3 - 8x^2) = -4x^3 + 8x^2$ $\rightarrow (5x^2 - 2x^3) - (4x^3 - 8x^2) = 5x^2 - 2x^3 - 4x^3 + 8x^2$ Now combine like terms: $5x^2 - 2x^3 - 4x^3 + 8x^2 = -6x^3 + 13x^2$

Your Turn!		
	1) $(x^2 - 2x) + (2x^2 - 5) =$ _____	2) $(9x^3 + 3x) - (x^3 + 3) =$ _____
	3) $(x^2 - 7x) + (2x^2 - 4) =$ _____	4) $(9x^2 - 3) - (4x^2 + 2) =$ _____
	5) $(5x^2 + 3) - (4 - 3x^2) =$ _____	6) $(x^3 + x^2) - (x^3 - 8) =$ _____
	7) $(7x^3 - 3x) - (x - x^3) =$ _____	8) $(x - 3x^4) - (2x^4 + 7x) =$ _____
	9) $(6x^3 + 3) - (4 - 2x^3) =$ _____	10) $(7x^2 + 3x^3) - (9x^3 + 4) =$ _____

Find more at

bit.ly/2KUqHqQ

Topic	Multiplying Binomials
Notes	✓ A binomial is a polynomial that is the sum or the difference of two terms, each of which is a monomial. ✓ To multiply two binomials, use "FOIL" method. (First–Out–In–Last) $$(x + a)(x + b) = x \times x + x \times b + a \times x + a \times b = x^2 + bx + ax + ab$$
Example	**Multiply.** $(x - 3)(x + 7) =$ **Solution:** Use "FOIL". (First–Out–In–Last): $(x - 3)(x + 7) =$ $x^2 + 7x - 3x - 21$ Then simplify: $x^2 + 7x - 3x - 21 = x^2 + 4x - 21$
Your Turn!	1) $(x + 3)(x + 3) =$ _____ 2) $(x + 5)(x + 3) =$ _____ 3) $(x - 2)(x + 6) =$ _____ 4) $(x - 5)(x - 7) =$ _____ 5) $(x + 9)(x + 4) =$ _____ 6) $(x + 6)(x + 8) =$ _____ 7) $(x - 7)(x - 5) =$ _____ 8) $(x - 6)(x - 6) =$ _____ 9) $(x + 9)(x - 4) =$ _____ 10) $(x - 8)(x + 3) =$ _____

Find more at

bit.ly/3aCsOFL

Topic	**Multiplying and Dividing Monomials**
Notes	✓ When you divide or multiply two monomials you need to divide or multiply their coefficients and then divide or multiply their variables. ✓ In case of exponents with the same base, you need to subtract their powers. ✓ Exponent's rules: $$x^a \times x^b = x^{a+b}, \qquad \frac{x^a}{x^b} = x^{a-b}$$ $$\frac{1}{x^b} = x^{-b}, \quad (x^a)^b = x^{a \times b}$$ $$(xy)^a = x^a \times y^a$$
Example	**Divide expressions.** $\frac{-16x^4y^5}{2xy^2} =$ **Solution:** Use exponents' division rule: $\frac{x^a}{x^b} = x^{a-b}, \frac{x^4}{x} = x^{4-1} = x^3$ and $\frac{y^5}{y^2} = y^3$ Then: $\frac{-16x^4y^5}{2xy^2} = -8x^3y^3$
Your Turn! **Find more at** bit.ly/2WHp4Q4	1) $(x^5y)(xy^2) =$ _____ 2) $(x^6y^2)(x^2y^5) =$ _____ 3) $(x^6y^4)(2x^5y^3) =$ _____ 4) $(4x^3y^4)(4x^6y^6) =$ _____ 5) $(-7x^5y^7)(6x^6y^8) =$ _____ 6) $(-6x^8y^3)(9x^7y^4) =$ _____ 7) $\frac{48x^7y^6}{8x^5y^2} =$ _____ 8) $\frac{-54x^{12}y^{15}}{9x^8y^6} =$ _____

Topic	Multiplying a Polynomial and a Monomial
Notes	✓ When multiplying monomials, use the product rule for exponents. $x^a \times x^b = x^{a+b}$ ✓ When multiplying a monomial by a polynomial, use the distributive property. $$a \times (b + c) = a \times b + a \times c = ab + ac$$ $$a \times (b - c) = a \times b - a \times c = ab - ac$$
Example	*Multiply expressions.* $3x(4x - 3) =$ **Solution:** Use Distributive Property: $3x(4x - 3) = 3x \times 4x - 3x \times (3) =$ Now, simplify: $3x \times 4x - 3x \times (3) = 12x^2 - 9x$

Your Turn!

1) $2x(x + 3y) =$

_____

2) $x(x - 7y) =$

_____

3) $-x(4x - 6y) =$

_____

4) $5x(x + 7y) =$

_____

5) $-x(3x + 9y) =$

_____

6) $7x(5x - 7y) =$

_____

7) $-3x(x^3 + 2y^2 - 9x) =$

_____

8) $8x(x^2 - 5y^2 + 7) =$

_____

Topic	**Multiplying Monomials**
Notes	✓ A monomial is a polynomial with just one term: Examples: $5x$ or $7x^2yz^8$. ✓ When you multiply monomials, first multiply the coefficients (a number placed before and multiplying the variable) and then multiply the variables using multiplication property of exponents. $x^a \times x^b = x^{a+b}$
Example	***Multiply.*** $(-5xy^5z^5) \times (2x^2y^4z^6) =$ **Solution:** Multiply coefficients and find same variables and use multiplication property of exponents: $x^a \times x^b = x^{a+b}$ $-5 \times 2 = -10$, $x \times x^2 = x^{1+2} = x^3$, $y^5 \times y^4 = y^{5+4} = y^9$, and $z^5 \times z^6 = z^{5+6} = z^{11}$ Then: $(-5xy^5z^5) \times (2x^2y^4z^6) = -10x^3y^9z^{11}$

Your Turn!	1) $6x^2 \times 3x^4 =$ _____	2) $7x^8 \times 3x^4 =$ _____
	3) $-6x^2y^5 \times 7x^3y^6 =$ _____	4) $-4x^7y \times 3x^4y^3 =$ _____
	5) $6x^6y^5 \times 5x^3y^4 =$ _____	6) $-5x^6y^5 \times (-9x^8y^4) =$ _____
Find more at bit.ly/2KLVoP8	7) $12x^9y^8z^6 \times 4x^4y^5z =$ _____	8) $-8x^9y^7z^{10} \times 6x^4y^9z^5 =$ _____

Topic	Factoring Trinomials
Notes	To factor trinomial, use of the following methods: ✓ "FOIL": $(x + a)(x + b) = x^2 + (b + a)x + ab$ ✓ "Difference of Squares": $$a^2 - b^2 = (a + b)(a - b)$$ $$a^2 + 2ab + b^2 = (a + b)(a + b)$$ $$a^2 - 2ab + b^2 = (a - b)(a - b)$$ ✓ "Reverse FOIL": $x^2 + (b + a)x + ab = (x + a)(x + b)$
Example	**Factor this trinomial.** $x^2 + 12x + 35 =$ **Solution:** Break the expression into groups: $(x^2 + 5x) + (7x + 35)$ Now factor out x from $x^2 + 5x : x(x + 5)$, and factor out 7 from $7x + 35$: $7(x + 5)$ Then: $(x^2 + 5x) + (7x + 35) = x(x + 5) + 7(x + 5)$ Now factor out like term: $(x + 5) \rightarrow (x + 5)(x + 7)$
Your Turn!	1) $x^2 + 4x - 5 =$ _____ 2) $x^2 - x - 6 =$ _____ 3) $x^2 + 4x - 32 =$ ____ 4) $x^2 - 9x + 14 =$ _____ 5) $x^2 + 10x + 24 =$ _____ 6) $x^2 + 17x + 72 =$ _____ 7) $x^2 + 18x + 45 =$ _____ 8) $x^2 - 15x + 56 =$ _____

Find more at

bit.ly/38EpdJA

Chapter 10: Answers

Simplifying Polynomials

1) $-5x + 2$

2) $8x + 18$

3) $8x^2 - 20x$

4) $12x^2 + 42x$

5) $-12x^2$

6) $-47x^2 + 10x$

7) $x^2 + 6x + 5$

8) $x^2 + 14x + 48$

9) $8x^3 + 9x^2$

10) $-3x^5 + 9x^4$

Adding and Subtracting Polynomials

1) $3x^2 - 2x - 5$

2) $8x^3 + 3x - 3$

3) $3x^2 - 7x - 4$

4) $5x^2 - 5$

5) $8x^2 - 1$

6) $x^2 + 8$

7) $8x^3 - 4x$

8) $-5x^4 - 6x$

9) $8x^3 - 1$

10) $-6x^3 + 7x^2 - 4$

Multiplying Binomials

1) $x^2 + 6x + 9$

2) $x^2 + 8x + 15$

3) $x^2 + 4x - 12$

4) $x^2 - 12x + 35$

5) $x^2 + 13x + 36$

6) $x^2 + 14x + 48$

7) $x^2 - 12x + 35$

8) $x^2 - 12x + 36$

9) $x^2 + 5x - 36$

10) $x^2 - 5x - 24$

Multiplying and Dividing Monomials

1) $x^6 y^3$

2) $x^8 y^7$

3) $2x^{11} y^7$

4) $16x^9 y^{10}$

5) $-42x^{11} y^{15}$

6) $-54x^{15} y^7$

7) $6x^2 y^4$

8) $-6x^4 y^9$

Multiplying a Polynomial and a Monomial

1) $2x^2 + 6xy$

2) $x^2 - 7xy$

3) $-4x^2 + 6xy$

4) $5x^2 + 35xy$

5) $-3x^2 - 9xy$

6) $35x^2 - 49xy$

7) $-3x^4 - 6xy^2 + 27x^2$

8) $8x^3 - 40xy^2 + 56x$

Multiplying Monomials

1) $18x^6$

2) $21x^{12}$

3) $-42x^5y^{11}$

4) $-12x^{11}y^4$

5) $30x^9y^9$

6) $45x^{14}y^9$

7) $48x^{13}y^{13}z^7$

8) $-48x^{13}y^{16}z^{15}$

Factoring Trinomials

1) $(x+5)(x-1)$

2) $(x-3)(x+2)$

3) $(x-4)(x+8)$

4) $(x-7)(x-2)$

5) $(x+6)(x+4)$

6) $(x+8)(x+9)$

7) $(x+15)(x+3)$

8) $(x-7)(x-8)$

CHAPTER

11 Geometry and Solid Figures

Math topics that you'll learn in this chapter:

- ✓ The Pythagorean Theorem
- ✓ Complementary and Supplementary angles
- ✓ Parallel Lines and Transversal
- ✓ Triangles
- ✓ Special Right Triangles
- ✓ Polygons
- ✓ Circles
- ✓ Cubes
- ✓ Trapezoids
- ✓ Rectangle Prisms
- ✓ Cylinder

Topic	The Pythagorean Theorem
Notes	✓ In any right triangle: $a^2 + b^2 = c^2$
Example	Right triangle ABC (not shown) has two legs of lengths $9\ cm$ (AB) and $12\ cm$ (AC). What is the length of the third side (BC)? **Solution:** Use Pythagorean Theorem: $a^2 + b^2 = c^2$ Then: $a^2 + b^2 = c^2 \rightarrow 9^2 + 12^2 = c^2 \rightarrow 81 + 144 = c^2$ $c^2 = 225 \rightarrow c = \sqrt{225} = 15\ cm$

Your Turn!

1) _____

4 ? 3

2) _____

16 20 ?

3) _____

15 9 ?

4) _____

13 ? 12

Find more at

bit.ly/37Jl08v

Topic	**Complementary and Supplementary Angles**
Notes	✓ Complementary angles are two angles with a sum of $90°$. A common case is when they form a right angle. ✓ Supplementary angles are two angles with a sum of $180°$. A common case is when they lie on the same side of a straight line. $60°$ $30°$ $130°$ $50°$

Example	**Find the missing angle.** $x =?$ $43°$ **Solution:** Notice that two angles form a straight angle when together. This means that the angles are supplementary and have a sum of $180°$. $x + 43 = 180 \rightarrow x = 180 - 43 = 137°$

Your Turn! **Find more at** bit.ly/3nlOn6G	***Find the missing measurement in the pair of angles.***

1) $x =$ ___	2) $x =$ ___
$114°$ $x =?$	$55°$ $x =?$

Topic	Parallel lines and Transversals

Notes	✓ When a line (transversal) intersects two parallel lines in the same plane, eight angles are formed. In the following diagram, a transversal intersects two parallel lines. Angles 1, 7, 3, and 5 are congruent. Angles 2, 8, 4, and 6 are also congruent.
	✓ In the following diagram, the following angles are supplementary angles (their sum is 180):
	  - Angles 1 and 8
	  - Angles 2 and 7
	  - Angles 3 and 6
	  - Angles 4 and 5

Example	**In the following diagram, two parallel lines are cut by a transversal. What is the value of** x**?** **Solution:** The two angles 75° and $11x - 2$ are equal. $11x - 2 = 75$ Now, solve for x: $11x - 2 + 2 = 75 + 2 \rightarrow$ $11x = 77 \rightarrow x = \dfrac{77}{11} \rightarrow x = 7$
Your Turn! Find more at bit.ly/3yQMjsK	1) Find the measure of the angle indicated. $? = $ ___ 2) Solve for x. $x = $ ___ $100°$ $?$ $x + 139$ $132°$

Topic	**Triangles**
Notes	✓ In any triangle the sum of all angles is 180 degrees. ✓ Area of a triangle = $\frac{1}{2}(base \times height)$
Example	**What *is the area of the following triangle?*** **Solution:** Use the area formula: Area $= \frac{1}{2}(base \times height)$ $base = 12$ and $height = 8$ Area $= \frac{1}{2}(12 \times 8) = \frac{96}{2} = 48$

Your Turn!	1) _____	2) _____
Find more at bit.ly/3haZrRg	3) _____	4) _____

Topic	**Special Right Triangles**
Notes	✓ A special right triangle is a triangle whose sides are in a particular ratio. Two special right triangles are $45° − 45° − 90°$ and $30° − 60° − 90°$ triangles. ✓ In a special $45° − 45° − 90°$ triangle, the three angles are $45°$, $45°$ and $90°$. The lengths of the sides of this triangle are in the ratio of $1:1:\sqrt{2}$. ✓ In a special triangle $30° − 60° − 90°$, the three angles are $30° − 60° − 90°$. The lengths of this triangle are in the ratio of $1:\sqrt{3}:2$.
Example	*Find the length of the hypotenuse of a right triangle if the length of the other two sides are both 5 inches.* *Solution:* this is a right triangle with two equal sides. Therefore, it must be a $45° − 45° − 90°$ triangle. Two equal sides are 5 inches. *So,* **t**he length of the hypotenuse is $5\sqrt{2}$ inches. If the first and second value of the ratio $x:x:x\sqrt{2}$. $$x:x:x\sqrt{2} \rightarrow x = 5 \rightarrow 5:5:5\sqrt{2}$$
Your Turn! **Find more at** bit.ly/3xL9bJR	**Find the value of x and y in each triangle.** 1) $x = $ ___ $y = $ ___ 2) $x = $ ___ $y = $ ___

Topic	Polygons
Notes	Perimeter of a square $= 4 \times side = 4s$ Perimeter of a rectangle $= 2(width + length)$ Perimeter of trapezoid $= a + b + c + d$ Perimeter of a regular hexagon $= 6a$ Perimeter of a parallelogram $= 2(l + w)$

| **Example** | **Find the perimeter of following regular hexagon.**

 Solution: Since the hexagon is regular, all sides are equal. Then: Perimeter of Hexagon $= 6 \times (one\ side)$
 Perimeter of Hexagon $= 6 \times (one\ side) = 6 \times 7 = 42\ m$ |

Your Turn!

1) *(rectangle)* _____

7 in
13 in

2) *(trapezoid)* _____

7 m
9 m   9 m
12 m

3) *(regular hexagon)* ____

8 m

4) *(parallelogram)* _____

8 in
14 in

Topic	Circles
Notes	✓ In a circle, variable r is usually used for the radius and d for diameter and π is about 3.14. ✓ $Area\ of\ a\ circle = \pi r^2$ ✓ $Circumference\ of\ a\ circle = 2\pi r$ r
Example	**Find the area of the circle.** **Solution:** Use area formula: $Area = \pi r^2$ $r = 3\ in \rightarrow Area = \pi(3)^2 = 9\pi, \pi = 3.14$ **Then:** $Area = 9 \times 3.14 = 28.26\ in^2$ $3\ in$
Your Turn!	**Find the area of each circle.** ($\pi = 3.14$) 1) _____ $4\ cm$ 2) _____ $12\ in$ **Find the Circumference of each circle.** ($\pi = 3.14$) 3) _____ $6\ cm$ 4) _____ $11\ m$

Find more at

bit.ly/3nJdOP2

Topic	Cubes
Notes	✓ A cube is a three-dimensional solid object bounded by six square sides. ✓ Volume is the measure of the amount of space inside of a solid figure, like a cube, ball, cylinder or pyramid. ✓ Volume of a cube $= (one\ side)^3$ ✓ surface area of cube $= 6 \times (one\ side)^2$
Example	**Find the volume and surface area of the following cube.** 15 cm **Solution:** Use volume formula: $volume = (one\ side)^3$ Then: $volume = (one\ side)^3 = (15)^3 = 3,375\ cm^3$ Use surface area formula: $surface\ area\ of\ cube: 6(one\ side)^2 = 6(15)^2 = 6(225) = 1,350\ cm^2$
Your Turn!	**Find the volume of each cube.**

1) _____

8 in

2) _____

11 ft

3) _____

15 cm

4) _____

22 m

Find more at

bit.ly/2M6PfOl

Topic	**Trapezoids**
Notes	✓ A quadrilateral with at least one pair of parallel sides is a trapezoid. ✓ Area of a trapezoid $= \frac{1}{2}h(b_1 + b_2)$
Example	*Calculate the area of the trapezoid.* **Solution:** Use area formula: $A = \frac{1}{2}h(b_1 + b_2)$ $b_1 = 8\ cm$, $b_2 = 12\ cm$ and $h = 14\ cm$ Then: $A = \frac{1}{2}(14)(12 + 8) = 7(20) = 140\ cm^2$

Your Turn!

1) _____

6 cm

4 cm

10 cm

2) _____

9 m

10 m

12 m

3) _____

8 ft

6 ft

16 ft

4) _____

9 cm

6 cm

14 cm

Find more at

bit.ly/3hpKACJ

Topic	**Rectangular Prisms**
Notes	✓ A solid 3-dimensional object which has six rectangular faces. ✓ Volume of a Rectangular prism $= Length \times Width \times Height$ $Volume = l \times w \times h$ $Surface\ area = 2(wh + lw + lh)$
Example	**Find the volume and surface area of rectangular prism.** **Solution:** Use volume formula: $Volume = l \times w \times h$ Then: $Volume = 4 \times 2 \times 6 = 48\ m^3$ Use surface area formula: $Surface\ area = 2(wh + lw + lh)$ Then: $Surface\ area = 2((2 \times 6) + (4 \times 2) + (4 \times 6))$ $= 2(12 + 8 + 24) = 2(44) = 88\ m^2$
Your Turn!	**Find the surface area of each Rectangular Prism.**

Your Turn! section:

1) _____

5 ft
8 ft
3 ft

2) _____

7 cm
14 cm
6 cm

3) _____

10 m
15 m
10 m

4) _____

16 in
14 in
12 in

Find more at

bit.ly/3nKm2GT

Topic	Cylinder
Notes	✓ A cylinder is a solid geometric figure with straight parallel sides and a circular or oval cross section. ✓ *Volume of Cylinder Formula* $= \pi(radius)^2 \times height$ $\pi = 3.14$ ✓ *Surface area of a cylinder* $= 2\pi r^2 + 2\pi rh$ *height* *radius*
Example	**Find the volume and Surface area of the follow Cylinder.** **Solution:** Use volume formula: $Volume = \pi(radius)^2 \times height$ Then: $Volume = \pi(4)^2 \times 10 = 16\pi \times 10 = 160\pi$ $\pi = 3.14$ **then:** $Volume = 160\pi = 502.4\ cm^3$ Use surface area formula: $Surface\ area = 2\pi r^2 + 2\pi rh$ **Then:** $2\pi(4)^2 + 2\pi(4)(10) = 2\pi(16) + 2\pi(40) = 32\pi + 80\pi = 112\pi$ $\pi = 3.14$ **Then:** $Surface\ area = 112 \times 3.14 = 351.68\ cm^2$ $10\ cm$ $4\ cm$
Your Turn!	**Find the volume of each Cylinder.** ($\pi = 3.14$) 1) _____ $7\ in$ $3\ in$ 2) _____ $11\ m$ $6\ m$ **Find the Surface area of each Cylinder.** ($\pi = 3.14$) 3) _____ $12\ ft$ $9\ ft$ 4) _____ $14\ cm$ $7\ cm$

Find more at

bit.ly/37LtcVM

Chapter 11: Answers

The Pythagorean Theorem

1) 5   3) 12

2) 12   4) 5

Complementary and Supplementary Angles

1) $66°$ 2) $35°$

Parallel lines and Transversals

1) $80°$ 2) -7

Triangles

1) 25   3) 330

2) 96   4) 640

Special Right Triangles

1) $x = 24 \ \ y = 12\sqrt{3}$ 2) $x = 7 \ \ y = 7\sqrt{2}$

Polygons

1) $40 \ in$ 3) $48 \ m$

2) $37 \ m$ 4) $44 \ in$

Circles

1) $50.24 \ cm^2$ 3) $37.68 \ cm$

2) $452.16 \ in^2$ 4) $69.08 \ m$

Cubes

1) $512 \ in^3$ 3) $3,375 \ cm^3$

2) $1,331 \ ft^3$ 4) $10,648 \ m^3$

Trapezoids

1) $32 \ cm^2$ 3) $72 \ ft^2$

2) $105 \ m^2$ 4) $69 \ cm^2$

Rectangle Prisms

    1) $158\ ft^2$ 3) $800\ m^2$

    2) $448\ cm^2$ 4) $1{,}168\ in^2$

Cylinder

    1) $197.82\ in^3$ 3) $1{,}186.92\ ft^2$

    2) $1{,}243.44\ m^3$ 4) $923.16\ cm^2$

CHAPTER

12 Statistics

Math topics that you'll learn in this chapter:

- ✓ Mean, Median, Mode, and Range of the Given Data
- ✓ Probability Problems
- ✓ Pie Graph
- ✓ Permutations and Combinations

95

Topic	Mean, Median, Mode, and Range of the Given Data
Notes	✓ Mean: $\frac{sum\ of\ the\ data}{total\ number\ of\ data\ entires}$ ✓ Mode: value in the list that appears most often. ✓ Median: is the middle number of a group of numbers that have been arranged in order by size. ✓ Range: the difference of largest value and smallest value in the list.
Example	**Find the mode and median of these numbers?** $18, 11, 6, 3, 1, 18, 2, 8$ **Solution:** Mode: value in the list that appears most often. Number 18 is the value in the list that appears most often (there are two number 18). To find median, write the numbers in order: $1, 2, 3, 6, 8, 11, 18, 18$ Number 6 and 8 are in the middle. Find their average: $\frac{6+8}{2} = \frac{14}{2} = 7$ The median is 7.

Your Turn!

1) $7, 6, 3, 8, 7, 5$

   Mode: _____   Range: _____

   Mean: _____   Median: _____

2) $6, 3, 2, 12, 8, 6, 5, 14$

   Mode: _____   Range: _____

   Mean: _____   Median: _____

3) $4, 9, 3, 1, 5, 4, 18, 12$

   Mode: _____   Range: _____

   Mean: _____   Median: _____

4) $12, 9, 8, 5, 9, 7, 4, 10$

   Mode: _____   Range: _____

   Mean: _____   Median: _____

Find more at

bit.ly/2KO86gg

Topic	Probability Problems
Notes	✓ Probability is the likelihood of something happening in the future. It is expressed as a number between zero (can never happen) to 1 (will always happen). ✓ Probability can be expressed as a fraction, a decimal, or a percent. ✓ Probability formula: $Probability = \frac{number\ of\ desired\ outcomes}{number\ of\ total\ outcomes}$
Example	***If there are 3 green balls, 4 red balls, and 10 blue balls in a basket, what is the probability that Jason will pick out a red ball from the basket?*** **Solution:** There are 4 red ball and 17 are total number of balls. Therefore, probability that Jason will pick out a red ball from the basket is 4 out of 17 or $\frac{4}{3+4+10} = \frac{4}{17}$
Your Turn! **Find more at** bit.ly/3phwk1p	1) A number is chosen at random from 1 to 12. Find the probability of selecting a prime number. (A prime number is a whole number that is only divisible by itself and 1) _____
	2) There are only red and blue cards in a box. The probability of choosing a red card in the box at random is one third. If there are 32 blue cards, how many cards are in the box? _____
	3) A die is rolled, what is the probability that an even number is obtained? _____

Topic	Pie Graph
Notes	✓ A Pie Chart is a circle chart divided into sectors; each sector represents the relative size of each value.
Example	A library has 420 books that include Mathematics, Physics, Chemistry, English and History. Use following graph to answer the question. **What is the number of Physics books?** **Solution:** Number of total books $= 420$ Percent of Physics books $= 25\% = 0.25$ Then, umber of Physics books: $$0.25 \times 420 = 105$$
Your Turn! **Find more at** bit.ly/34ECTDv	The circle graph below shows all Mr. Smith's expenses for last month. Mr. Smith spent \$520 for clothes last month. Mr. Smith's last month expenses 1) How much did Mr. Smith spend for his Books last month? _____ 2) How much did Mr. Smith spend for Bills last month? _____ 3) How much did Mr. Smith spend for his foods last month? _____

Topic	**Permutations and Combinations**
Notes	✓ Permutations: The number of ways to choose a sample of k elements from a set of n distinct objects where order does matter, and replacements are not allowed. For a permutation problem, use this formula: $$_nP_k = \frac{n!}{(n-k)!}$$ ✓ Combination: The number of ways to choose a sample of r elements from a set of n distinct objects where order does not matter, and replacements are not allowed. For a combination problem, use this formula: $$_nC_r = \frac{n!}{r!\,(n-r)!}$$ ✓ Factorials are products, indicated by an exclamation mark. For example, 4! Equals: $4 \times 3 \times 2 \times 1$. Remember that 0! is defined to be equal to 1.
Example	***How many ways can we pick a team of 5 people from a group of 8?*** **Solution:** Since the order doesn't matter, we need to use combination formula where n is 8 and r is 5. Then: $\frac{n!}{r!\,(n-r)!} = \frac{8!}{5!\,(8-5)!} = \frac{8!}{5!\,(3)!} = \frac{8 \times 7 \times 6 \times 5!}{5!\,(3)!} = \frac{8 \times 7 \times 6}{3 \times 2 \times 1} = \frac{56}{2} = 28$
Your Turn! **Find more at** bit.ly/34BQgUY	1) In how many ways can 7 athletes be arranged in a straight line? _____
	2) How many ways can we award a first and second place prize among seven contestants? _____
	3) In how many ways can we choose 3 players from a team of 9 players? _____

Chapter 12: Answers

Mean, Median, Mode, and Range of the Given data

1) Mode: 7   Range: 5   Mean: 6   Median: 6.5

2) Mode: 6   Range: 12   Mean: 7   Median: 6

3) Mode: 4   Range: 17   Mean: 7   Median: 4.5

4) Mode: 9   Range: 8   Mean: 8   Median: 8.5

Probability Problems

1) $\frac{5}{12}$ 2) 48   3) $\frac{1}{2}$

Pie Graph

1) $312   2) $520   3) $650

Permutations and Combinations

1) 5,040   2) 42   3) 84

13 Functions Operations

Math topics that you'll learn in this chapter:

- ✓ Function Notation and Evaluation
- ✓ Adding and Subtracting Functions
- ✓ Multiplying and Dividing Functions
- ✓ Composition of Functions

101

Topic	**Function Notation and Evaluation**
Notes	✓ Functions are mathematical operations that assign unique outputs to given inputs. ✓ Function notation is the way a function is written. It is meant to be a precise way of giving information about the function without a rather lengthy written explanation. ✓ The most popular function notation is $f(x)$ which is read "f of x". ✓ To evaluate a function, plug in the input (the given value or expression) for the function's variable (place holder, x).
Example	**Evaluate**: $h(n) = n^2 - 3$, find $h(4)$. **Solution:** Substitute n with 4: Then: $h(n) = n^2 - 3 \rightarrow h(4) = (4)^2 - 3 = 16 - 3 \rightarrow h(4) = 13$

Your Turn!		
	1) $f(x) = x - 5$, find $f(-4)$ _____	2) $g(x) = 4x + 2$, find $g(3)$ _____
	3) $g(n) = 6n - 4$, find $g(-2)$ _____	4) $h(n) = n^2 - 8$, find $h(-5)$ _____
	5) $f(x) = x^2 + 9$, find $f(-4)$ _____	6) $g(x) = 3x^2 - 7$, find $g(-6)$_____
	7) $w(x) = 4x^2 - x$, find $w(3n)$ _____	8) $p(x) = 3x^3 - 7$, find $p(-2a)$ _____

Find more at

bit.ly/3mls7lF

Topic	Adding and Subtracting Functions
Notes	✓ Just like we can add and subtract numbers and expressions, we can add or subtract two functions and simplify or evaluate them. The result is a new function. ✓ For two functions $f(x)$ and $g(x)$, we can create two new functions: $(f + g)(x) = f(x) + g(x)$ and $(f - g)(x) = f(x) - g(x)$
Example	$g(a) = 3a - 2$, $f(a) = a + 5$, **Find**: $(g + f)(a)$ **Solution**: $(g + f)(a) = g(a) + f(a)$ Then: $(g + f)(a) = (3a - 2) + (a + 5) = 4a + 3$

Your Turn!	
1) $g(x) = x - 6$ $h(x) = 2x + 4$ Find: $(h + g)(3)$ _____	2) $f(x) = 3x + 4$ $g(x) = -x - 8$ Find: $(f + g)(2)$ _____
3) $f(x) = 4x + 9$ $g(x) = 3x - 10$ Find: $(f - g)(-4)$ _____	4) $h(x) = 4x^2 - 6$ $g(x) = 2x + 11$ Find: $(h + g)(5)$ _____
5) $g(x) = 9x - 7$ $h(x) = 6x^2 + 10$ Find: $(h - g)(x)$ _____	6) $h(x) = -2x^2 - 18$ $g(x) = 3x^2 + 10$ Find: $(h - g)(a)$ _____

Topic	**Multiplying and Dividing Functions**
Notes	✓ Just like we can multiply and divide numbers and expressions, we can multiply and divide two functions and simplify or evaluate them. ✓ For two functions $f(x)$ and $g(x)$, we can create two new functions: $(f.g)(x) = f(x).g(x)$ and $\left(\dfrac{f}{g}\right)(x) = \dfrac{f(x)}{g(x)}$
Example	$g(x) = x + 9, f(x) = x - 2$, Find: $(g.f)(3)$ **Solution:** $(g.f)(x) = g(x).f(x) = (x+9)(x-2) = x^2 - 2x + 9x - 18 = x^2 + 7x - 18$ Substitute x with 3: $(g.f)(x) = (3)^2 + 7(3) - 18 = 9 + 21 - 18 = 12$

Your Turn!	1) $g(x) = x - 5$ $h(x) = x + 3$ Find: $(g.h)(4)$ ————	2) $f(x) = x + 6$ $g(x) = -x - 6$ Find: $\left(\dfrac{f}{g}\right)(-2)$ ————
	3) $f(x) = 3x + 6$ $g(x) = 2x - 7$ Find: $\left(\dfrac{f}{g}\right)(4)$ ————	4) $h(x) = x^2 - 8$ $g(x) = x + 4$ Find: $(g.h)(-3)$ ————
Find more at bit.ly/3ph7kHA	5) $g(x) = 5x - 9$ $h(x) = x^2 - 6$ Find: $(g.h)(-3)$ ————	6) $h(x) = 4x^2 - 7$ $g(x) = -3x - 9$ Find: $\left(\dfrac{h}{g}\right)(-2)$ ————

Topic	Composition of Functions
Notes	✓ "Composition of functions" simply means combining two or more functions in a way where the output from one function becomes the input for the next function. ✓ The notation used for composition is: $(fog)(x) = f(g(x))$ and is read "f composed with g of x" or "f of g of x".
Example	**Using $f(x) = x - 4$ and $g(x) = x + 1$, find: $(fog)(4)$** **Solution:** $(fog)(x) = f(g(x))$ Then: $(fog)(x) = f(g(x)) = f(x + 1) = x + 1 - 4 = x - 3$ Substitute x with 4: $(fog)(4) = f(g(4)) = 4 - 3 = 1$

Your Turn!	1) $f(x) = 2x$ $g(x) = x + 3$ Find: $(fog)(2)$ ————	2) $f(x) = x + 5$ $g(x) = x - 7$ Find: $(fog)(-2)$ ————
	3) $f(x) = 4x$ $g(x) = x + 5$ Find: $(gof)(4)$ ————	4) $h(x) = x - 2$ $g(x) = 3x + 4$ Find: $(goh)(2)$ ————
Find more at bit.ly/2WHBkAg	5) $f(x) = 4x - 2$ $g(x) = x + 9$ Find: $(fog)(-1)$ ————	6) $f(x) = x^2 - 3$ $g(x) = 3x - 5$ Find: $(gof)(2)$ ————

Chapter 13: Answers

Function Notation and Evaluation

1) -9

2) 14

3) -16

4) 17

5) 25

6) 101

7) $36n^2 - 3n$

8) $-24a^3 - 7$

Adding and Subtracting Functions

1) 7

2) 0

3) 15

4) 115

5) $6x^2 - 9x + 17$

6) $-5a^2 - 28$

Multiplying and Dividing Function

1) -7

2) -1

3) 18

4) 1

5) -72

6) -3

Composition of Function

1) 10

2) -4

3) 21

4) 4

5) 30

6) -2

Time to Test

Time to refine your Math skills with a practice test

In this section, there are two complete PERT Mathematics Tests. Take these tests to simulate the test day experience. After you've finished, score your test using the answer key.

Before You Start

- You'll need a pencil, a timer, and a four-function calculator to take the test.

- Use the answer sheet provided to record your answers. (You can cut it out or photocopy it)

- For each question there are four possible answers. Choose which one is best.

- After you've finished the test, review the answer key to see where you went wrong and what areas you need to improve.

Good Luck!

PERT Mathematics
Practice Test 1

2023 - 2024

Total number of questions: 30

Total time (Calculator): No time limit

You may use a calculator on this Test.

109

PERT Mathematics Practice Test Answer Sheet

Remove (or photocopy) this answer sheet and use it to complete the practice test.

	PERT Mathematics Practice Test 1 Answer Sheet		
1	Ⓐ Ⓑ Ⓒ Ⓓ	13 Ⓐ Ⓑ Ⓒ Ⓓ	25 Ⓐ Ⓑ Ⓒ Ⓓ
2	Ⓐ Ⓑ Ⓒ Ⓓ	14 Ⓐ Ⓑ Ⓒ Ⓓ	26 Ⓐ Ⓑ Ⓒ Ⓓ
3	Ⓐ Ⓑ Ⓒ Ⓓ	15 Ⓐ Ⓑ Ⓒ Ⓓ	27 Ⓐ Ⓑ Ⓒ Ⓓ
4	Ⓐ Ⓑ Ⓒ Ⓓ	16 Ⓐ Ⓑ Ⓒ Ⓓ	28 Ⓐ Ⓑ Ⓒ Ⓓ
5	Ⓐ Ⓑ Ⓒ Ⓓ	17 Ⓐ Ⓑ Ⓒ Ⓓ	29 Ⓐ Ⓑ Ⓒ Ⓓ
6	Ⓐ Ⓑ Ⓒ Ⓓ	18 Ⓐ Ⓑ Ⓒ Ⓓ	30 Ⓐ Ⓑ Ⓒ Ⓓ
7	Ⓐ Ⓑ Ⓒ Ⓓ	19 Ⓐ Ⓑ Ⓒ Ⓓ	
8	Ⓐ Ⓑ Ⓒ Ⓓ	20 Ⓐ Ⓑ Ⓒ Ⓓ	
9	Ⓐ Ⓑ Ⓒ Ⓓ	21 Ⓐ Ⓑ Ⓒ Ⓓ	
10	Ⓐ Ⓑ Ⓒ Ⓓ	22 Ⓐ Ⓑ Ⓒ Ⓓ	
11	Ⓐ Ⓑ Ⓒ Ⓓ	23 Ⓐ Ⓑ Ⓒ Ⓓ	
12	Ⓐ Ⓑ Ⓒ Ⓓ	24 Ⓐ Ⓑ Ⓒ Ⓓ	

1) In the triangle below, if the measure of angle A is 37 degrees, then what is the value of y?

(figure is NOT drawn to scale)

A. 62

B. 70

C. 78

D. 86

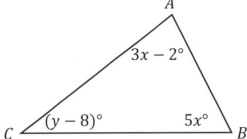

2) Simplify the expression.

$$(6x^3 - 8x^2 + 2x^4) - (4x^2 - 2x^4 + 2x^3)$$

A. $4x^4 + 4x^3 - 12x^2$

B. $4x^3 - 12x^2$

C. $4x^4 + 8x^3 - 12x^2$

D. $8x^3 - 12x^2$

Questions 3 to 5 are based on the following data

Types of air pollutions in 10 cities of a country

3) If a is the mean (average) of the number of cities in each pollution type category, b is the mode, and c is the median of the number of cities in each pollution type category, then which of the following must be true?

A. $a < b < c$

B. $b < a < c$

C. $a = c$

D. $b < c = a$

4) What percent of cities are in the type of pollution A, C, and D respectively?

A. $60\%, 40\%, 90\%$

B. $30\%, 40\%, 90\%$

C. $30\%, 40\%, 60\%$

D. $40\%, 60\%, 90\%$

5) How many cities should be added to type of pollutions B until the ratio of cities in type of pollution B to cities in type of pollution E will be 0.625?

A. 2

B. 3

C. 4

D. 5

6) There are only red and blue cards in a box. The probability of choosing a red card in the box at random is one third. If there are 246 blue cards, how many cards are in the box?

A. 123

B. 308

C. 328

D. 369

7) $\frac{1}{6b^2} + \frac{1}{6b} = \frac{1}{b^2}$, then $b = ?$

 A. $-\frac{16}{15}$

 B. 5

 C. $-\frac{15}{16}$

 D. 8

8) In two successive years, the population of a town is increased by 15% and 20%. What percent of the population is increased after two years?

 A. 32%

 B. 35%

 C. 38%

 D. 68%

9) Which of the following graphs represents the compound inequality $-2 \le 2x - 4 < 8$?

 A.

 B.

 C.

 D.

10) What is the volume of a box with the following dimensions?

   Height = 4 *cm*   Width = 5 *cm*   Length = 6 *cm*

   A. 15 cm^3

   B. 60 cm^3

   C. 90 cm^3

   D. 120 cm^3

11) In the diagram below, circle A represents the set of all odd numbers, circle B represents the set of all negative numbers, and circle C represents the set of all multiples of 5. Which number could be replaced with y?

   A. 5

   B. 0

   C. −5

   D. −10

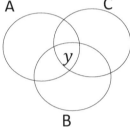

12) A basket contains 20 balls and the average weight of each of these balls is 25 *g*. The five heaviest balls have an average weight of 40 *g* each. If we remove the five heaviest balls from the basket, what is the average weight of the remaining balls?

   A. 10

   B. 20

   C. 30

   D. 35

13) Mr. Carlos family are choosing a menu for their reception. They have 3 choices of appetizers, 5 choices of entrees, 4 choices of cake. How many different menu combinations are possible for them to choose?

   A. 12

   B. 32

   C. 60

   D. 120

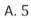

14) In a stadium the ratio of home fans to visiting fans in a crowd is $5:7$. Which of the following could be the total number of fans in the stadium?

   A. 12,324

   B. 42,326

   C. 44,566

   D. 66,812

15) Last week 24,000 fans attended a football match. This week three times as many bought tickets, but one sixth of them cancelled their tickets. How many are attending this week?

   A. 48,000

   B. 54,000

   C. 60,000

   D. 72,000

16) What is the perimeter of a square in centimeters that has an area of $595.36 \ cm^2$?

   A. 97.6

   B. 96.2

   C. 95.7

   D. 92.6

17) A bread recipe calls for $2\frac{2}{3}$ cups of flour. If you only have $2\frac{5}{6}$ cups, how much more flour is needed?

   A. 1

   B. $\frac{1}{2}$

   C. 2

   D. $\frac{5}{6}$

18) The perimeter of a rectangular yard is 60 meters. What is its length if its width is twice its length?

A. 10 meters

B. 18 meters

C. 20 meters

D. 24 meters

19) Which of the following shows the numbers in increasing order?

$$\frac{2}{3}, 0.68, 67\%, \frac{4}{5}$$

A. $67\%, 0.68, \frac{2}{3}, \frac{4}{5}$

B. $67\%, 0.68, \frac{4}{5}, \frac{2}{3}$

C. $0.68, 67\%, \frac{2}{3}, \frac{4}{5}$

D. $\frac{2}{3}, 67\%, 0.68, \frac{4}{5}$

20) The mean of 50 test scores was calculated as 88. But it turned out that one of the scores was misread as 94 but it was 69. What is the correct mean of the test scores?

A. 85

B. 87

C. 87.5

D. 88.5

21) If Jim adds 100 stamps to his current stamp collection, the total number of stamps will be equal to $\frac{6}{5}$ the current number of stamps. If Jim adds 50% more stamps to the current collection, how many stamps will be in the collection?

A. 150

B. 300

C. 600

D. 750

22) Two dice are thrown simultaneously, what is the probability of getting a sum of 6 or 9?

   A. $\frac{1}{3}$

   B. $\frac{1}{4}$

   C. $\frac{1}{6}$

   D. $\frac{1}{12}$

23) A swimming pool holds 2,000 cubic feet of water. The swimming pool is 25 feet long and 10 feet wide. How deep is the swimming pool?

   A. 2

   B. 4

   C. 6

   D. 8

24) What is the area of a square whose diagonal is 8?

   A. 16

   B. 32

   C. 36

   D. 64

25) The sum of 8 numbers is greater than 240 and less than 320. Which of the following could be the average (arithmetic mean) of the numbers?

   A. 30

   B. 35

   C. 40

   D. 45

26) Anita's trick–or–treat bag contains 12 pieces of chocolate, 18 suckers, 18 pieces of gum and 24 pieces of licorice. If she randomly pulls a piece of candy from her bag, what is the probability of her pulling out a piece of sucker?

   A. $\frac{1}{3}$

   B. $\frac{1}{4}$

   C. $\frac{1}{6}$

   D. $\frac{1}{12}$

27) The average of 6 numbers is 12. The average of 4 of those numbers is 10. What is the
average of the other two numbers?

    A. 10

    B. 12

    C. 14

    D. 16

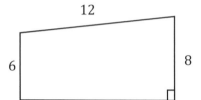

28) In the following figure, point Q lies on line n, what is the value of y if $x = 35$?

    A. 15

    B. 25

    C. 35

    D. 45

29) The perimeter of the trapezoid below is $36\ cm$. What is its area?

    A. $576\ cm^2$

    B. $70\ cm^2$

    C. $48\ cm^2$

    D. $24\ cm^2$

30) If 150% of a number is 75, then what is the 90% of that number?

    A. 45

    B. 50

    C. 70

    D. 85

IF YOU FINISH BEFORE TIME IS CALLED, YOU MAY CHECK YOUR WORK ON THIS TEST.

STOP

PERT Mathematics
Practice Test 2
2023 - 2024

Total number of questions: 30

Total time (Calculator): No time limit

You may use a calculator on this Test.

119

PERT Mathematics Practice Test Answer Sheet

Remove (or photocopy) this answer sheet and use it to complete the practice test.

PERT Mathematics Practice Test 2 Answer Sheet

1	Ⓐ Ⓑ Ⓒ Ⓓ	13	Ⓐ Ⓑ Ⓒ Ⓓ	25	Ⓐ Ⓑ Ⓒ Ⓓ
2	Ⓐ Ⓑ Ⓒ Ⓓ	14	Ⓐ Ⓑ Ⓒ Ⓓ	26	Ⓐ Ⓑ Ⓒ Ⓓ
3	Ⓐ Ⓑ Ⓒ Ⓓ	15	Ⓐ Ⓑ Ⓒ Ⓓ	27	Ⓐ Ⓑ Ⓒ Ⓓ
4	Ⓐ Ⓑ Ⓒ Ⓓ	16	Ⓐ Ⓑ Ⓒ Ⓓ	28	Ⓐ Ⓑ Ⓒ Ⓓ
5	Ⓐ Ⓑ Ⓒ Ⓓ	17	Ⓐ Ⓑ Ⓒ Ⓓ	29	Ⓐ Ⓑ Ⓒ Ⓓ
6	Ⓐ Ⓑ Ⓒ Ⓓ	18	Ⓐ Ⓑ Ⓒ Ⓓ	30	Ⓐ Ⓑ Ⓒ Ⓓ
7	Ⓐ Ⓑ Ⓒ Ⓓ	19	Ⓐ Ⓑ Ⓒ Ⓓ		
8	Ⓐ Ⓑ Ⓒ Ⓓ	20	Ⓐ Ⓑ Ⓒ Ⓓ		
9	Ⓐ Ⓑ Ⓒ Ⓓ	21	Ⓐ Ⓑ Ⓒ Ⓓ		
10	Ⓐ Ⓑ Ⓒ Ⓓ	22	Ⓐ Ⓑ Ⓒ Ⓓ		
11	Ⓐ Ⓑ Ⓒ Ⓓ	23	Ⓐ Ⓑ Ⓒ Ⓓ		
12	Ⓐ Ⓑ Ⓒ Ⓓ	24	Ⓐ Ⓑ Ⓒ Ⓓ		

1) In a scale diagram, 0.15 inch represents 150 feet. How many inches represent 2.5 feet?

   A. 0.001 in

   B. 0.012 in

   C. 0.0025 in

   D. 0.002 in

2) If $\frac{3}{7}$ of Z is 54, what is $\frac{2}{5}$ of Z?

   A. 44.2

   B. 46.3

   C. 48.4

   D. 50.4

3) Mary has 8 blue pens, 2 green pens, and 4 black pens. If she picks out one pen randomly, what is the probability that she picks a blue pen?

   A. $\frac{3}{7}$

   B. $\frac{4}{7}$

   C. $\frac{5}{7}$

   D. $\frac{6}{7}$

4) A car travels at a speed of 72 miles per hour. How far will it travel in 8 hours?

   A. 574 miles

   B. 576 miles

   C. 578 miles

   D. 580 miles

5) If Sam spent $60 on sweets and he spent 25% of the selling price for the tip, how much did he spend?

   A. $66

   B. $69

   C. $72

   D. $75

6) Which of the following numbers has factors that include the smallest factor (other than 1)

of 95?

A. 28

B. 32

C. 39

D. 45

7) $\frac{4^2+3^2+(-5)^2}{(9+10-11)^2}=?$

A. $\frac{25}{32}$

B. 56

C. -56

D. $-\frac{25}{32}$

8) Angle A and angle B are supplementary. The measure of angle A is 2 times the measure of

angle B. What is the measure of angle A in degrees?

A. $100°$

B. $120°$

C. $140°$

D. $160°$

9) $200(3 + 0.01)^2 - 200 =?$

A. 201.55

B. 361.08

C. 702.88

D. 1,612.02

10) If $x = -2$ in the following equation, what is the value of y? $2x + 3 = \frac{y+6}{5}$

A. -9

B. -11

C. -13

D. -15

11) Tomas is 6 feet 8.5 inches tall, and Alex is 5 feet 3 inches tall. What is the difference in height, in inches, between Alex and Tomas?

A. 2.5

B. 7.5

C. 12.5

D. 17.5

12) What is the solution to $\frac{0.02}{0.25} = \frac{1.25}{x}$?

A. 0.150

B. 1.156

C. 11.565

D. 15.625

13) The least of 8 consecutive integers is m, and the greatest is n. What is the value of $\frac{m+n}{3}$ in terms of m?

A. $m + 1$

B. $2m + 8$

C. $\frac{2m+7}{3}$

D. $\frac{2m}{7}$

14) In the infinitely repeating decimal below, 1 is the first digit in the repeating pattern. What is the 68th digit? $\frac{1}{7} = 0.\overline{142857}$

A. 1

B. 2

C. 4

D. 7

15) Yesterday Kylie writes 10% of her homework. Today she writes another 18% of the entire homework. What fraction of the homework is left for her to write?

  A. $\frac{7}{25}$

  B. $\frac{4}{25}$

  C. $\frac{18}{25}$

  D. $\frac{10}{25}$

16) In a box of blue and yellow pens, the ratio of yellow pens to blue pens is $2:3$. If the box contains 9 blue pens, how many yellow pens are there?

  A. 3

  B. 4

  C. 5

  D. 6

17) What decimal is equivalent to $-\frac{6}{9}$?

  A. $-0.\overline{5}$

  B. $-0.\overline{6}$

  C. $-0.\overline{65}$

  D. $-0.\overline{7}$

18) How many positive even factors of 68 are greater than 26 and less than 60?

  A. 0

  B. 1

  C. 2

  D. 6

19) Simplify: $-11.6 + 6.7 - 2(-15.3)$

    A. 19.7

    B. 21.7

    C. 23.7

    D. 25.7

20) The ratio of two sides of a parallelogram is $2:3$. If its perimeter is $40\ cm$, find the length of its sides.

    A. $8\ cm, 12\ cm$

    B. $10\ cm, 14\ cm$

    C. $12\ cm, 16\ cm$

    D. $14\ cm, 18\ cm$

21) If x can be any integer, what is the greatest possible value of the expression $2 - x^2$?

    A. -1

    B. 0

    C. 3

    D. 2

22) A store has a container of handballs: 6 green, 5 blue, 8 white, and 10 yellow. If one ball is picked from the container at random, what is the probability that it will be green?

    A. $\frac{1}{5}$

    B. $\frac{6}{11}$

    C. $\frac{6}{29}$

    D. $\frac{8}{25}$

23) In the figure below, F is the midpoint of EH. Which segment has length $2y - x$ centimeters?

    A. EF

    B. GH

    C. EG

    D. FH

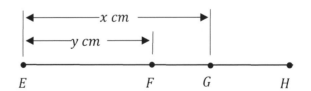

24) 12 Students had a mean score of 75. The remaining 10 students of the class had an average score of 85. What is approximately the mean (average) score of the entire class?

A. 73.5

B. 75.5

C. 77.5

D. 79.5

25) For what value of x is the equation $\frac{x}{4} - 2.5 = 4(6 - 3x) - 2$ true?

A. 0.5

B. 1.8

C. 2

D. 3.4

26) If $x = 3$, what is the approximate value of the following expression? $4x^3 + 2x + \frac{1}{x^2} + 8$

A. 112

B. 115.2

C. 122.1

D. 132.3

27) The probability of drawing a blue candy at random from a bag of 30 candies is $\frac{3}{5}$. After 6 blue candies are removed from the bag, what is the probability of randomly drawing a blue candy from the bag?

A. $\frac{1}{4}$

B. $\frac{1}{2}$

C. $\frac{3}{5}$

D. 1

28) Emma answered 9 out of 45 questions on a test incorrectly. What percentage of the questions did she answer correctly?

    A. 10%

    B. 40%

    C. 68%

    D. 80%

29) $9 - 2(4n + 7) - (5n + 9) = ?$

    A. $-30n - 14$

    B. $-13n - 14$

    C. $-25n - 1$

    D. $-31n - 14$

30) If Anna multiplies her age by 5 and then adds 3, she will get a number equal to her mother's age. If x is her mother's age, what is Anna's age in terms of x?

    A. $\frac{x-3}{5}$

    B. $\frac{x-5}{3}$

    C. $3x + 5$

    D. $5x - 3$

IF YOU FINISH BEFORE TIME IS CALLED, YOU MAY CHECK YOUR WORK ON THIS TEST. STOP

PERT Mathematics Practice Test Answers

Now, it's time to review your results to see where you went wrong and what areas you need to improve!

PERT Math Practice Test 1				PERT Math Practice Test 2			
1	D	21	D	1	C	21	D
2	A	22	B	2	D	22	C
3	C	23	D	3	B	23	B
4	A	24	B	4	B	24	D
5	A	25	B	5	D	25	C
6	D	26	B	6	D	26	C
7	B	27	D	7	A	27	B
8	C	28	B	8	B	28	D
9	D	29	B	9	D	29	B
10	D	30	A	10	B	30	A
11	C			11	D		
12	B			12	D		
13	C			13	C		
14	A			14	C		
15	C			15	C		
16	A			16	D		
17	D			17	B		
18	A			18	B		
19	D			19	D		
20	C			20	A		

PERT Mathematics Practice Test Answers and Explanations

PERT Mathematics Practice Test 1

1)   Choice D is correct

In the figure angle A is labeled $(3x - 2)$ and it measures 37. Thus, $3x - 2 = 37$ and $3x = 39$ or $x = 13$. That means that angle B, which is labeled $(5x)$, must measure $5 \times 13 = 65$.

Since the three angles of a triangle must add up to 180,

$37 + 65 + y - 8 = 180$, then: $y + 94 = 108 \rightarrow y = 180 - 94 = 86$

2)   Choice A is correct

Simplify and combine like terms.

$(6x^3 - 8x^2 + 2x^4) - (4x^2 - 2x^4 + 2x^3) \Rightarrow (6x^3 - 8x^2 + 2x^4) - 4x^2 + 2x^4 - 2x^3 \Rightarrow$

$4x^4 + 4x^3 - 12x^2$

3)   Choice C is correct

Let's find the mean (average), mode and median of the number of cities for each type of pollution. Number of cities for each type of pollution: $6, 3, 4, 9, 8$

$$average\ (mean) = \frac{sum\ of\ terms}{number\ of\ terms} = \frac{6+3+4+9+8}{5} = \frac{30}{5} = 6$$

The Median is the number in the middle. To find median, first list numbers in order from smallest to largest. $3, 4, 6, 8, 9$. The median of the data is 6.

Mode is the number which appears most often in a set of numbers. Therefore, there is no mode in the set of numbers. Median = Mean, then, $a = c$

4)   Choice A is correct

Percent of cities in the type of pollution A: $\frac{6}{10} \times 100 = 60\%$

Percent of cities in the type of pollution C: $\frac{4}{10} \times 100 = 40\%$

Percent of cities in the type of pollution D: $\frac{9}{10} \times 100 = 90\%$

5) Choice A is correct

Let the number of cities should be added to type of pollutions B be x. Then:

$$\frac{x+3}{8} = 0.625 \rightarrow x + 3 = 8 \times 0.625 \rightarrow x + 3 = 5 \rightarrow x = 2$$

6) Choice D is correct

Let x be total number of cards in the box, then number of red cards is: $x - 246$

The probability of choosing a red card is one third. Then: $probability = \frac{1}{3} = \frac{x-132}{x}$

Use cross multiplication to solve for x.

$$x \times 1 = 3(x - 246) \rightarrow x = 3x - 738 \rightarrow 2x = 738 \rightarrow x = 369$$

7) Choice B is correct

Subtract $\frac{1}{6b}$ and $\frac{1}{b^2}$ from both sides of the equation. Then:

$$\frac{1}{6b^2} + \frac{1}{6b} = \frac{1}{b^2} \rightarrow \frac{1}{6b^2} - \frac{1}{b^2} = -\frac{1}{6b}$$

Multiply both numerator and denominator of the fraction $\frac{1}{b^2}$ by 6. Then:

$$\frac{1}{6b^2} - \frac{6}{6b^2} = -\frac{1}{6b}$$

Simplify the first side of the equation: $-\frac{5}{6b^2} = -\frac{1}{6b}$

Use cross multiplication method: $30b = 6b^2 \rightarrow 30 = 6b \rightarrow b = 5$

8) Choice C is correct

The population is increased by 15% and 20%. 15% increase changes the population to 115% of original population. For the second increase, multiply the result by 120%.

$(1.15) \times (1.20) = 1.38 = 138\%$. 38 percent of the population is increased after two years.

9) Choice D is correct

Solve for x. $-2 \leq 2x - 4 < 8 \Rightarrow$ (add 4 all sides) $-2 + 4 \leq 2x - 4 + 4 < 8 + 4 \Rightarrow$

$2 \leq 2x < 12 \Rightarrow$ (divide all sides by 2) $1 \leq x < 6$

x is between 1 and 6. Choice D represent this inequality.

10) Choice D is correct

Use Volume of a box formula: $length \times width \times height = 4 \times 5 \times 6 = 120$

11) Choice C is correct

y is the intersection of the three circles. Therefore, it must be odd (from circle A), negative (from circle B), and multiple of 5 (from circle C).

From the choices provided, only -5 is odd, negative and multiple of 5.

12) Choice B is correct

Recall that the formula for the average is: $Average = \dfrac{sum\ of\ data}{number\ of\ data}$

First, compute the total weight of all balls in the basket: $25\ g = \dfrac{total\ weight}{20\ balls}$

$25\ g \times 20 = total\ weight = 500\ g$. Next, find the total weight of the 5 largest marbles:

$40\ g = \dfrac{total\ weight}{5\ marbles} \rightarrow 40\ g \times 5 = total\ weight = 200\ g$

The total weight of the heaviest balls is $200\ g$. Then, the total weight of the remaining 15 balls is $300\ g$. $500\ g - 200\ g = 300\ g$.

The average weight of the remaining balls: $Average = \dfrac{300\ g}{15\ marbles} = 20\ g$ per ball

13) Choice C is correct

To find the number of possible outfit combinations, multiply number of options for each factor:

$3 \times 5 \times 4 = 60$

14) Choice A is correct

In the stadium the ratio of home fans to visiting fans in a crowd is $5:7$. Therefore, total number of fans must be divisible by $12: 5 + 7 = 12$.

Let's review the choices:

A. $12,324 \rightarrow 12,324 \div 12 = 1,027$

B. $42,326 \rightarrow 42,326 \div 12 = 3,527.166$

C. $44,566 \rightarrow 44,566 \div 12 = 3,713.833$

D. $66,812 \rightarrow 66,812 \div 12 = 5,567.666$

Only choice A when divided by 12 results a whole number.

15) Choice C is correct

Three times of 24,000 is 72,000. One sixth of them cancelled their tickets.

One sixth of 72,000 equals $12,000(\frac{1}{6} \times 72,000 = 12,000)$.

$60,000(72,000 - 12,000 = 60,000)$ fans are attending this week.

16) Choice A is correct

The area of the square is 595.36. Therefore, the side of the square is square root of the area.

$\sqrt{595.36} = 24.4$

Four times the side of the square is the perimeter: $4 \times 24.4 = 97.6$

17) Choice D is correct

Fist convert mixed numbers to fractions: $2\frac{2}{3} - 1\frac{5}{6} = 2\frac{4}{6} - 1\frac{5}{6} = \frac{16}{6} - \frac{11}{6} = \frac{5}{6}$

18) Choice A is correct

The width of the rectangle is twice its length. Let x be the length. Then, width$= 2x$

Perimeter of the rectangle is 2 (width + length) $= 2(2x + x) = 60 \Rightarrow 6x = 60 \Rightarrow x = 10$

Length of the rectangle is 10 meters.

19) Choice D is correct

Change the numbers to decimal and then compare.

$$\frac{2}{3} = 0.666$$

$$0.68$$

$$67\% = 0.67$$

$$\frac{4}{5} = 0.80$$

Then: $\frac{2}{3} < 67\% < 0.68 < \frac{4}{5}$

20) Choice C is correct

$$average \ (mean) = \frac{sum \ of \ terms}{number \ of \ terms} \Rightarrow 88 = \frac{sum \ of \ terms}{50} \Rightarrow sum = 88 \times 50 = 4,400$$

The difference of 94 and 69 is 25. Therefore, 25 should be subtracted from the sum.

$$4,400 - 25 = 4,375$$

$$mean = \frac{sum \ of \ terms}{number \ of \ terms} \Rightarrow mean = \frac{4,375}{50} = 87.5$$

21) Choice D is correct

Let x be the number of current stamps in the collection. Then:

$$\frac{6}{5}x - x = 100 \rightarrow \frac{1}{5}x = 100 \rightarrow x = 500$$

50% more of 500 is: $500 + 0.50 \times 500 = 500 + 250 = 750$

22) Choice B is correct

To get a sum of 6 for two dice, we can get 5 different options: $(5, 1), (4, 2), (3, 3), (2, 4), (1, 5)$

To get a sum of 9 for two dice, we can get 4 different options: $(6, 3), (5, 4), (4, 5), (3, 6)$

Therefore, there are 9 options to get the sum of 6 or 9.

Since, we have $6 \times 6 = 36$ total options, the probability of getting a sum of 6 and 9 is 9 out of 36 or $\frac{1}{4}$.

23) Choice D is correct

Use formula of rectangle prism volume.

$V = (length)(width)(height) \Rightarrow 2,000 = (25)(10)(height) \Rightarrow height = 2,000 \div 250 = 8$

24) Choice B is correct

The diagonal of the square is 8. Let x be the side.

Use Pythagorean Theorem: $a^2 + b^2 = c^2$

$x^2 + x^2 = 8^2 \Rightarrow 2x^2 = 8^2 \Rightarrow 2x^2 = 64 \Rightarrow x^2 = 32 \Rightarrow x = \sqrt{32}$

The area of the square is: $\sqrt{32} \times \sqrt{32} = 32$

25) Choice B is correct

The sum of 8 numbers is greater than 240 and less than 320. Then, the average of the 8 numbers must be greater than 30 and less than 40.

$\frac{240}{8} < x < \frac{320}{8} \rightarrow 30 < x < 40$

The only choice that is between 30 and 40 is 35.

26) Choice B is correct

Probability $= \dfrac{number\ of\ desired\ outcomes}{number\ of\ total\ outcomes} = \dfrac{18}{12+18+24} = \dfrac{18}{72} = \dfrac{1}{4}$

27) Choice D is correct

Use the average formula: average $= \dfrac{sum\ of\ terms}{number\ of\ terms} \Rightarrow$ (average of 6 numbers)

$12 = \dfrac{sum\ of\ numbers}{6} \Rightarrow$ sum of 6 numbers is $12 \times 6 = 72$

(Average of 4 numbers) $10 = \dfrac{sum\ of\ numbers}{4} \Rightarrow$ sum of 4 numbers is $10 \times 4 = 40$

Sum of 6 numbers − sum of 4 numbers = sum of 2 numbers $72 - 40 = 32$

Average of 2 numbers $= \frac{32}{2} = 16$

28) Choice B is correct

The angles on a straight line add up to 180 degrees. Then: $x + 25 + y + 2x + y = 180$

Then, $3x + 2y = 180 - 25 \rightarrow 3(35) + 2y = 155 \rightarrow 2y = 155 - 105 = 50 \rightarrow y = 25$

29) Choice B is correct

The perimeter of the trapezoid is $36\ cm$

Therefore, the missing side (height) is $= 36 - 8 - 12 - 6 = 10$

Area of a trapezoid: $A = \frac{1}{2}h(b_1 + b_2) = \frac{1}{2}(10)(6 + 8) = 70$

30) Choice A is correct

First, find the number. Let x be the number. Write the equation and solve for x.

150% of a number is 75, then: $1.5 \times x = 75 \Rightarrow x = 75 \div 1.5 = 50$

90% of 50 is: $0.9 \times 50 = 45$

PERT Mathematics Practice Test 2

1) Choice C is correct

Let x be the number of inches representing 2.5 feet. Set up a proportion and solve for x:

$$\frac{x}{2.5} = \frac{0.15}{150} \rightarrow x = \frac{0.15 \times 2.5}{150} \rightarrow x = 0.0025 \, in$$

2) Choice D is correct

Set an equation: $\frac{3}{7}Z = 54$

Solve for Z: $\rightarrow Z = 54 \times \frac{7}{3} = 126$, then, calculate $\frac{2}{5}Z$: $\frac{2}{5} \times 126 = 50.4$

3) Choice B is correct

The number of pens is 14. The probability of picking a blue pen is: $\frac{8}{14} = \frac{4}{7}$

4) Choice B is correct

To answer this question, multiply 72 miles per hour to $8 \rightarrow 72 \times 8 = 576$ miles

5) Choice D is correct

The spent amount is $60, and the tip is 25%. Then: $tip = 0.25 \times 60 = \$15$

Final price = Selling price + tip $\rightarrow$ final price = $60 + \$15 = \$75$

6) Choice D is correct

To find the smallest factor of 95, list the factors: $1, 5, 19,$ and 95. The smallest factor (other than 1)

is 5. Of the choices listed $(28, 32, 39,$ and $45)$, only 45 is a multiple of 5.

7) Choice A is correct

1) Adding exponents is done by calculating each exponent first and then adding and dividing:

$$\frac{4^2 + 3^2 + (-5)^2}{(9 + 10 - 11)^2} = \frac{16 + 9 + 25}{(8)^2} = \frac{50}{64} = \frac{25}{32}$$

8) Choice B is correct

Angle A and angle B are supplementary, so the sum of their angles is $180°$.

Let a equal the measure of angle A, and let b equal the measure of angle B.

$a + b = 180$

The measure of angle A is 2 times the measure of angle B.

$$a = 2b \rightarrow 2b + b = 180 \rightarrow 3b = 180 \rightarrow b = \frac{180}{3} = 60$$

$$a = 2b = 2(60) = 120$$

Therefore, the measure of angle A is $120°$.

9) Choice D is correct

First calculate exponents value, then multiplying and subtracting:

$200(3 + 0.01)^2 - 200 = 200(3.01)^2 - 200 = 200(9.06) - 200 = 1,612.02$

10) Choice B is correct

Substitute -2 for x in the equation: $2(-2) + 3 = \frac{y+6}{5} \rightarrow -1 = \frac{y+6}{5} \rightarrow y + 6 = -5 \rightarrow$

$y = -5 - 6 = -11$

11) Choice D is correct

First, convert their heights from feet and inches to inches, by multiplying the number of feet by 12 and adding the inches. Tomas: 6 feet $+8.5$ inches. $6(12$ inches$) +8.5$ inches$= 72$ inches $+8.5$ inches $= 80.5$ inches. Alex: 5 feet $+3$ inches. $5(12$ inches$)+3$ inches $= 60$ inches$+3$ inches $= 63$ inches

Then, subtract Alex's height from Tomas's height: $80.5 - 63 = 17.5$

12) Choice D is correct

To eliminate the decimals in this equation, multiply the numerators and denominators by 100:

$\left(\frac{0.02}{0.25}\right)\left(\frac{100}{100}\right) = \left(\frac{1.25}{x}\right)\left(\frac{100}{100}\right) \rightarrow \left(\frac{2}{25}\right) = \frac{125}{100x} \rightarrow x = \left(\frac{125}{100}\right)\left(\frac{25}{2}\right) = 15.625$

13) Choice C is correct

The first integer is m, so the second is $m + 1$, the rest are $m + 2, m + 3, m + 4, m + 5, m + 6$ and finally $m + 7$. Since n is the eight and greatest of the integers, $n = m + 7$.

Substitute $m + 7$ for n and simplify: $\frac{m+n}{3} = \frac{m+m+7}{3} = \frac{2m+7}{3}$

14) Choice C is correct

There are 6 digits in the repeating decimal (0.142857), so digit 1 would be the first, seventh, thirteenth digit and so on. To find the 68th digit, divide 68 by 6.

$68 \div 6 = 11r2$

Since the remainder is 2, that means the 68th digit is the same as the 2^{ed} digit, which is 4.

15) Choice C is correct

So far, Kylie has written $10\% + 18\% = 28\%$ of the entire homework. That means she has $100\% - 28\% = 72\%$ left to write. $72\% = \frac{72}{100} = \frac{18}{25}$

16) Choice D is correct

Let x be the number of yellow pens. Write a proportion and solve: $\frac{yellow}{blue} = \frac{2}{3} = \frac{x}{9}$

Solve the equation: $18 = 3x \rightarrow x = 6$

17) Choice B is correct

To find the decimal equivalent to $-\frac{6}{9}$, divide 6 by 9. Then:

$$-\frac{6}{9} = -0.66666\ldots = -0.\overline{6}$$

18) Choice B is correct

List the factors of 68: 1 and 68, 2 and 34, 4 and 17. There is one factor greater than 26 and less than 60.

19) Choice D is correct

First multiply 2 and -15.3. Then, calculate the result.

$$-11.6 + 6.7 - 2(-15.3) = -11.6 + 6.7 + 30.6 = 25.7$$

20) Choice A is correct

Let the lengths of two sides of the parallelogram be $2x\ cm$ and $3x\ cm$ respectively. Then, its perimeter $= 2(2x + 3x) = 10x$

Therefore, $10x = 40 \rightarrow x = 4$

One side $= 2(4) = 8\ cm$ and other side is: $3(4) = 12\ cm$

21) Choice D is correct

To answer this question, assign several positive and negative values to x and determine what the value of the expression will be:

x	-2	-1	0	1	2
$2 - x^2$	-2	1	2	1	-2

So, the maximum value of the expression is 2.

22) Choice C is correct

The total number of handballs in the container is $6 + 5 + 8 + 10 = 29$. Since there are 6 green handballs, the probability of selecting a green handball is $\frac{6}{29}$

23) Choice B is correct

These facts are given: F is the midpoint of EH.

EG has a length of x cm. EF has a length of y cm.

Use the first two facts to determine that E has a length of $2y$ centimeters:

$$GH = EH - EG = 2y - x$$

24) Choice D is correct

Total score of first 12 students $= 12 \times 75 = 900$

Total score of remaining 10 students $= 10 \times 85 = 850$

Mean score of the whole class $= \frac{900 + 850}{22} \approx 79.5$

25) Choice C is correct

Apply the distributive property; multiply 4 by 6 and $-3x$:

$\frac{x}{4} - 2.5 = 24 - 12x - 2$. Simplify: $\frac{x}{4} - 2.5 = 22 - 12x$

Apply the additive inverse property; add $12x$ and 2.5 to both sides of the equation:

$\frac{x}{4} + 12x = 24.5$. Get a common denominator: $\frac{x + 48x}{4} = 24.5$

Apply the multiplicative inverse property; multiply both sides of the equation by 4:

$49x = 98$. Divide both sides of the equation by 49: $x = \frac{98}{49} = 2$

26) Choice C is correct

Substitute 3 for x:

$$4(3^3) + 2(3) + \frac{1}{(3)^2} + 8 = 108 + 6 + \frac{1}{9} + 8 = 122 + \frac{1}{9} = \frac{1,099}{9} \approx 122.1$$

27) Choice B is correct

Start with a proportion to determine the total number of blue candies in the bag.

$$\frac{3}{5} = \frac{r}{30} \rightarrow \frac{3}{5}(30) = r \rightarrow r = 18$$

There are currently 18 blue candies out of 30 candies in the bag. After 6 blue candies are removed, there would be 12 blue candies left in the bag and 24 total candies.

The probability of randomly drawing a blue candy would then be $\frac{12}{24} = \frac{1}{2}$

28) Choice D is correct

If Emma answered 9 out of 45 questions incorrectly, then she answered 36 questions correctly.

$$\frac{36}{45} \times 100 = 80\%$$

29) Choice B is correct

First multiply 2 by $4n$ and 7: $9 - 8n - 14 - 5n - 9$. Then, combine like terms:

$$9 - 8n - 14 - 5n - 9 = -13n - 14$$

30) Choice A is correct

Let y be Anna's age:

$$5y + 3 = x \rightarrow 5y = x - 3 \rightarrow y = \frac{x-3}{5}$$

Receive the PDF version of this book or get another FREE book!

Thank you for using our Book!

Do you LOVE this book?

Then, you can get the PDF version of this book or another book absolutely FREE!

Please email us at:

info@EffortlessMath.com

for details.

Author's Final Note

I hope you enjoyed reading this book. You've made it through the book! Great job!

First of all, thank you for purchasing this study guide. I know you could have picked any number of books to help you prepare for your PERT Math test, but you picked this book and for that I am extremely grateful.

It took me years to write this study guide for the PERT Math because I wanted to prepare a comprehensive PERT Math study guide to help test takers make the most effective use of their valuable time while preparing for the test.

After teaching and tutoring math for over a decade, I've gathered my personal notes and lessons to develop this study guide. It is my greatest hope that the lessons in this book could help you prepare for your test successfully.

If you have any questions, please contact me at reza@effortlessmath.com and I will be glad to assist. Your feedback will help me to greatly improve the quality of my books in the future and make this book even better. Furthermore, I expect that I have made a few minor errors somewhere in this study guide. If you think this to be the case, please let me know so I can fix the issue as soon as possible.

If you enjoyed this book and found some benefit in reading this, I'd like to hear from you and hope that you could take a quick minute to post a review on the book's Amazon page. To leave your valuable feedback, please visit: amzn.to/3gGc8Ui

Or scan this QR code.

I personally go over every single review, to make sure my books really are reaching out and helping students and test takers. Please help me help PERT Math test takers, by leaving a review!

I wish you all the best in your future success!

Reza Nazari

Math teacher and author

Made in United States
Orlando, FL
06 February 2023